THE BETTER HALF OF LIFE

Also by Jean Shaw . . .
Second Cup of Coffee

THE BETTER HALF OF LIFE

OF LIFE

Meditations
From Ecclesiastes

JEAN SHAW

Zondervan Publishing House
Grand Rapids, Michigan

Daybreak Books are published by the Zondervan Publishing House
1415 Lake Drive, S.E., Grand Rapids, Michigan 49506

Library of Congress Cataloging in Publication Data
Shaw, Jean
  The better half of life.
    1. Bible. O.T. Ecclesiastes—Meditations. 2. Women—Religious life.
I. Bible O.T. Ecclesiastes. English. New International. Selections. 1983
II. Title.
BS1475.4.S53   1983   242'.643   82-16088
ISBN 0-310-43621-4

In many instances, feminine pronouns are used with generic meaning
and are not intended to exclude men.

All Scripture quotations, unless otherwise noted, are taken from the
HOLY BIBLE: NEW INTERNATIONAL VERSION (North American Edi-
tion). Copyright © 1973, 1978, 1984, by the International Bible Society.
Used by permission of Zondervan Bible Publishers.

Psalter portions are from *The Book of Psalms for Singing*, copyright ©
1973 by the Board of Education and Publication, Reformed Presbyterian
Church of North America, Pittsburg, Pennsylvania. Used by permission.

Edited by James E. Ruark
Designed by Kim Koning and James E. Ruark

Printed in the United States of America

88   89   90   91   92   93 / CH / 10   9   8   7   6   5   4   3   2

To my husband, Gordon

However many years we may live,
we will enjoy them all.

Preface

The two-story house on the corner is draped in black. Leftover flowers from our local mortuary are arranged across the front lawn. Hanging from the balcony is a large sign: "Denise Carter Is 40 Today." Denise's three teen-agers have expressed their perspective about turning forty. Denise accepts the joke in good humor—and goes off to play second base for the Manchester Bulldogs.

When you are fifteen, forty appears to be death itself. When you're forty, life seems to be just getting under way. You finally have a handle on things. The children are relatively independent. You own all your major appliances. You know what your husband likes for dinner and what makes him angry. You've accepted the fact that he will never give up the green plaid shirt he got in college, or his habit of leaving his shoes under the coffee table.

With life spans now reaching into the eighties, forty seems to be a good point for dividing life into its first and second halves. Is the second half really better? Perhaps you see it as a time to launch forth into a whole sea of new experiences. You can go back to school, or to work, take a trip without the children, or join the growing number of women who are having a baby and just getting into the whole child-raising process!

Or perhaps you see the second half of life as decidedly gloomy. You're going to be lonely. You'll be making more visits to the doctor. One day will be just like another. Even a face-lift won't hide the fact that you are no longer thirty-five.

Ecclesiastes has a message for those who have turned the corner, but are not yet over the hill. To the optimist and pessimist alike, the Teacher—"Koheleth"—brings words of wisdom that offer perspective and stability at the time in life when we need them most.

The book, like its Author, is realistic. It admits to the problems of aging. But it offers a surprising note of encouragement, too. If you are not convinced that getting older can be a blessing, take a little time each day to study Ecclesiastes. "The end of the matter is better than its beginning" can be a truth that will add an expectant note to each day.

THE BETTER HALF OF LIFE

"Meaningless! Meaningless!" says the Teacher. "Utterly meaningless! Everything is meaningless" (1:2).

These could be the words of a man poised to jump from a twelfth-story window. Life has been a series of disasters, and the future promises no change of fortune. "What is the purpose of living?" he asks. "Everything is meaningless."

At a less dramatic, but more common level, there comes a point in midlife when we survey what we have accomplished so far and despair at our own insignificance. There is little satisfaction in possessions. The last time we moved I looked at the van in the driveway and realized that everything we own could be fitted into a vehicle forty-two feet long.

If things do not give meaning to our existence, perhaps we can rejoice in what we have done. But here, too, there is the possibility of despair. We didn't become vice-president of the company. We never painted the great picture, or were elected to city council, or became famous for our blueberry pie. The dreams of youth will never be fulfilled. Here we are, fifty years old, and life seems to be on "hold."

Yet, in this very verse that seems to be a charge against God, there lies a reason for praise. The value of my life does *not* depend on what I own or what I have done. In light of how little that is, I can rejoice! The more so when I understand that were I to have the wealth of an Arabian sheik and the prestige of the president of the United States, life could still be meaningless. It will certainly end.

Only in my relationship to God is there any purpose in life. As He is my father, so I am His child and important to Him. Everything I do is significant. "He does not take his eyes off the righteous," we read in Job 36:7. "He enthrones them with kings and exalts them forever."

If it was never intended that I reach royal heights in this life, God knows and God cares. He never takes His eyes off

9

me. "Cast all your anxiety on him because he cares for you," says 1 Peter 5:7. Every minute of this life is meaningful. So what if I don't attain greatness or wealth? In the next life God promises me that I shall sit with kings.

> At all times I will bless the LORD
> In praise my mouth employ;
> My soul shall in Jehovah boast;
> The meek shall hear with joy.
> O magnify the LORD with me;
> Let us exalt His name.
> In all my fears I sought the LORD;
> From Him deliv'rance came.
>
> Psalm 34:1–4

What does man gain from all his labor at which he toils under the sun? (1:3).

It was a lovely luncheon, with the whole office present. Mr. Weygand made a speech about Betty's thirty years of loyal service to Weygand Associates. Mr. Barnes presented her with a powder-blue set of luggage and an airline ticket to Boston to visit her sister. There were handshakes and kissing, "Best wishes!" and "We'll miss you!" Betty cleaned out her desk, said her final good-bys, and drove home from the company parking lot for the last time.

Thirty years with Weygand had produced a comfortable two-bedroom house, completely paid for. There was a three-year-old car and a modest investment program. With Social Security and retirement benefits, Betty would be able to live comfortably, if not lavishly. Still, the recent TV special about people on a fixed income kept upsetting Betty's attempt at confidence. Words like "double-digit inflation," "high-risk commodities," and "eroding buying power" turned up in every discussion about senior citizens.

Betty had just assumed that her lifelong labor would provide for her old age. She hadn't expected luxury, but she certainly didn't want to be dependent on anyone. What was the good of working so hard if you had to worry every time you sat down to pay your fuel bill?

Why do we work? It certainly makes play more appreciated! Basically, of course, we work to provide for our needs. Charles Kingsley's famous quotation points out other values: "Thank God every morning when you get up that you have something to do that day which must be done, whether you like it or not. Being forced to work, and forced to do your best, will breed in you temperance and self-control, diligence and strength of will, cheerfulness and content, and a hundred virtues which the idle never know."

11

Has your work developed in you certain qualities of character? Has it enabled you to help others? Through your work have you found friends? Led another to Christ?

Paul says in 1 Thessalonians 4:11–12: "Make it your ambition to lead a quiet life, to mind your own business and to work with your hands, just as we told you, so that your daily life may win the respect of outsiders and so that you will not be dependent on anybody."

Independence, then, is a goal God wants for us. But in acquiring it, we honor Him in other ways. How we work, and where, and with whom has an impact far beyond what we can imagine.

> *For some life's years are seventy;*
> > *Perhaps the strong may eighty see;*
> *Their best involves but toil and woe;*
> > *All quickly ends. How soon we go!*
> *Who has Thine anger understood?*
> *Who fears Thy fury as he should?*
>
> *O teach Thou us to count our days*
> > *And set our hearts on wisdom's ways.*
> *How long, O Lord? Return! Repent,*
> > *And toward Thy servants now relent.*
> *Each morning fill us with Thy grace;*
> *We'll sing for joy through all our days.*
> > Psalm 90:10–14

What has been will be again, what has been done will be done again; there is nothing new under the sun. Is there anything of which one can say, "Look! This is something new"? It was here already, long ago; it was here before our time (1:9–10).

The child who tries to stump dad with a riddle is always surprised to find out that dad used the same riddle on *his* father! A complaint about the wickedness of today's teenagers will usually prompt someone to dig out a well-known discourse on the same subject written by an ancient Greek. The Christian church is assaulted regularly with movements involving body life or discipling or missions that appear to be innovative, but actually go back to the New Testament.

Of course, there are new *inventions* under the sun. The Bible isn't talking about microwave ovens or computers—it's talking about people. People are basically the same, whether they lived in a cave or have just moved into a solar-energy earth house. A glove commercial on TV pictures Eve eating an apple: the significance of that first sinful experience in the Garden of Eden is entirely understandable to people today. Human nature doesn't change.

So much in life operates in cycles. Skirt lengths go up, only to go down. Educators divide up the country schoolhouse into many rooms, then tear down the walls and put all the children back together into learning pods. Childbirth moved from the bedroom to the hospital; now it is fashionable to have babies born at home. Nature sets the pattern with its cyclical courses. Like the earth, we are all in an orbit of one kind or another.

It is easy to lose our sense of surprise. What excites the young is old stuff to us. What concerns the new convert we dismiss with a "ho-hum." People and crises come and go, and we can't see any reason to make a big to-do about it.

Paul tells us in 2 Corinthians 5:17 that anyone who is in

Christ is a new creation: "The old has gone, the new has come!" And this newness is meant to last all our lives. "The LORD'S . . . compassions never fail. They are new every morning," we read in Lamentations 3:22–23.

We experience this in God's care for our needs. We feel it when He forgives our sins and restores our soul. We see it in the flicker who discovered our bird feeder this morning. Seeds are flying in all directions! Just when winter sameness was dragging us down, God sent the unexpected.

We can agree with the writer of Ecclesiastes. Flickers and forgiveness were here already, long ago. People are the same. But God's Holy Spirit, working in our lives, gives us a fresh perspective. As we grow up into Jesus, we see them all in a new way.

> *Sing a new song to Jehovah*
> *For the wonders He has wrought;*
> *His right hand and arm most holy*
> *Have to Him salvation brought.*
> Psalm 98:1

There is no remembrance of men of old, and even those who are yet to come will not be remembered by those who follow (1:11).

Picture yourself on stage in front of a television audience. The master of ceremonies smiles at you with his perfect teeth and exclaims, "Now—for ten thousand dollars, name the first man to set foot on the moon!" A huge clock begins to tick, its single hand marking the seconds like wedges of a giant pizza. You grope. You remember seeing the astronaut slowly descend the ladder from the spaceship and bounce into the dust. What was his name? Everybody talked about it—a man on the moon! You sweat. Your brain is a box of Styrofoam packing material. No answer comes, and the hand reaches sixty, sounding an alarm that denies you the financial windfall of a lifetime.

A screen at the back of the stage flashes the name "Neil Alden Armstrong," and you groan. Of course, that's who it was! Nineteen-sixty-nine. Not so very long ago, really. But you had forgotten. Take heart: a recent survey revealed that *most* Americans couldn't remember the name of the first man on the moon. And they weren't on national TV.

Heroes last a very short time. Nonheroes are forgotten, too. Can you name the last five vice-presidents of the United States? And the funny, bearded sidekick of the cowboy star—that was ...?

Will anyone remember me? Probably not. My memory is only as old as my youngest grandchild. The generation after that will think of me as a person in a photograph: "That's great-grandmother standing in her vegetable garden."

Whether people think of me after I die isn't all that important. The living have all they can manage keeping track of the living! I am happy knowing that God will always remember me. I am one of His people, and to us He says,

15

"Though the mountains be shaken and the hills be removed, yet my unfailing love for you will not be shaken or my covenant of peace be removed" (Isa. 54:10). Jesus has prepared a place for me in heaven—a room just for me! When I get there, He will know my name and acknowledge it before God and His angels (Rev. 3:5). There's an audience that really matters. TV can't even come close.

> The very steps of man have been
> Established by the LORD;
> He takes great pleasure in man's way,
> His progress to record.
>
> Though he may stumble, he shall not
> Fall so he cannot stand,
> Because Jehovah is the One
> Who holds him by his hand.
>
> I have been young, now many years
> Have o'er my life been spread;
> I've never seen the righteous left,
> His children begging bread.
>
> All day he's gracious and he lends;
> His sons a blessing are.
> Depart from evil, and do good,
> And dwell for evermore.
>
> Psalm 37:23–27

Then I applied myself to the understanding of wisdom, and also of madness and folly, but I learned that this, too, is a chasing after the wind. For with much wisdom comes much sorrow; the more knowledge, the more grief (1:17–18).

In his search for satisfaction, the writer of Ecclesiastes begins with wisdom. He *applies* himself—not a seminar here and a night course there, but deep study and exploration. If Israel University had offered a Ph.D., he would have earned one and gone on for postdoctoral research.

Since wisdom is so highly commended in other portions of scripture (see Prov. 1–3), we may admit to some confusion. Why is wisdom "chasing after the wind" here? The answer is in the kind of wisdom. We see no mention of spiritual wisdom, no reference to the fear of the Lord, which is the beginning of wisdom. "Much wisdom" is "the best thinking that man can do on his own" (Derek Kidner). It proves to be not only disappointing, but actually depressing.

Not that Christians are supposed to be uneducated. If we are to replenish and subdue the earth, we have to understand it. Adam and Eve had to know the habits of the creatures God had made. They had to learn farming. Our earth is photovoltaic cells, space shuttles, and genetic engineering. More than 300,000 home computers are doing everything from income taxes to dinner menus. The electronic marvel that was a figment of science-fiction imagination is now as common as the typewriter.

We can never stop learning. Whether we retire to a planned adult community or a mobile home, we have to cope with new technology. A task as basic as grocery shopping involves merchandising methods that will discourage and frighten us if we don't master them.

The necessity for learning how the world operates also acquaints us with its woes. The greater our knowledge of

17

mankind, the more intense our grief at the expansiveness of its sins. Television instantly informs us of the world's miseries. The prolonged process of a college education teaches us the more complex causes and effects.

Where can we find realism with satisfaction? "Preserve sound judgment and discernment," Solomon writes in Proverbs 3:21, 23–24. "Then you will go on your way in safety, and your foot will not stumble; when you lie down, you will not be afraid; when you lie down, your sleep will be sweet."

> I bless the LORD Who gives to me
> The counsel that is right;
> My heart within me He directs
> To teach me in the night.
>
> I've set the LORD before my face,
> And Him I'll always see.
> Because He stands at my right hand
> I never moved shall be.
>
> Because of this my heart is glad
> And joy shall be expressed
> By all my glory, and my flesh
> In confidence shall rest.
>
> Psalm 16:7–9

I thought in my heart, "Come now, I will test you with pleasure to find out what is good." But that also proved to be meaningless (2:1).

Since wisdom didn't make a meaningful life, our writer turns to pleasure. He tries cheering himself with wine— that fails—and embracing folly, i.e., having a good time. Ever the scientific investigator, he doesn't just plunge into any entertainment or sport. His mind guiding him with wisdom, he deliberately imitates what other people are doing. His neighbor owns a twenty-four-inch colored TV set with videotape equipment, remote-control tuner, and six electronic games. So he buys one, too.

As he munches his bag of corn chips while watching the thirty-fourth football game of the season, his exasperated wife stomps into the family room, turns off the TV, and cries, "I've had it! The whole house is falling apart and you sit there watching those stupid games!" She hands him a list of fix-it jobs and delivers the ultimatum: he gets to work or she gets out.

Reluctantly he rises from his favorite chair and goes down to the basement for a screwdriver to fix the storm door. He gets to thinking how nice a breezeway would be. He could connect it to the patio (have to rebuild that) and plant a garden. A small orchard would be pretty and provide fruit, too. Maybe a fish pond. Even a waterfall!

Soon he is the favorite customer at the hardware store. Building materials pile up in the garage. Trucks bearing cement, top soil, and railroad ties come and go. Two college students are hired to work all summer. The mayor offers a position on the park board. A fertilizer company arranges a lucrative contract for a commercial on TV.

It's immensely satisfying. The house looks fabulous. But when the work is all done, and there isn't an inch left for another improvement, our homeowner surveys the result of his labor and still feels empty. What has he gained, after all? In a few years the kids will move out. He and the wife will buy a smaller place. Nobody will remember his appearance on TV.

Where can our soul find satisfaction? The psalmist tells us in Psalm 107: " . . . give thanks to the LORD for his unfailing love and his wonderful deeds for men, for he satisfies the thirsty and fills the hungry with good things." Pleasure is for a moment. God's love is for ever and ever.

> O shout for joy unto the LORD,
> Earth's people far and near;
> With gladness serve the LORD; O come
> To Him with songs of cheer.

> Know that the LORD is God indeed;
> He made us; we are His.
> We are His people, and the sheep
> Kept where His pasture is.

> O enter then His gates with thanks,
> His courts with voice of praise;
> Give thanks to Him with joyfulness.
> And bless His name always.

> Because Jehovah is most good,
> His mercy never ends;
> And unto generations all
> His faithfulness extends.

> Psalm 100

I hated all the things I had toiled for under the sun, because I must leave them to the one who comes after me. And who knows whether he will be a wise man or a fool? Yet he will have control over all the work into which I have poured my effort and skill under the sun. This too is meaningless (2:18–19).

The Park seed catalogue advertises 113 years of dependable service—A FAMILY TRADITION. It began with George W. Park (born in 1852), went to Mary, then to George B., and then to William, president today. A portrait in the photography studio shows three nurses—obviously grandmother, mother, and daughter—each wearing her distinctive uniform and white cap. This morning's newspaper features an article about a four-generation farm; the present owner has been tilling its soil since 1950.

"Following in his father's footsteps" conjures up all kinds of pleasant pictures, doesn't it? The little child growing up with the family business. The proud moment when the signmaker adds & SON or & DAUGHTER to the name over the door. Great-grandpa Weatherly lying peacefully on his deathbed, knowing there is a fine young person in college, preparing to carry on the family enterprise.

But what if it doesn't turn out that way? Suppose the next in line is irresponsible. Or maybe he doesn't want to run the cement business—he wants to be a forest ranger instead. And what about the generation after that? No one can say for sure who will be minding the store.

Pouring all our effort and skill into our work so that we can pass it on to someone else is risky. We can minimize the problem by using investment counselors who will help us plan for the future. They will certainly recommend a will, a basic control over one's estate that is neglected by many people. There are myriad other more sophisticated plans that will guarantee the disposition of our funds to loved ones, our church, and Christian agencies. If we act now we can enjoy seeing some of our money go where we want it to.

As for the things we have toiled for, they may not be valued by those younger. The massive oak bedroom set is too large for an apartment. Nobody wants forty-five years of *Reader's Digest*, even in perfect condition with no issues missing. Even tactful rejection hurts. The more possessions we have, in fact, the greater our anxiety about what we are going to do with them when our world has shrunk to the dimensions of one room!

Paul reminds us in 1 Timothy 6:7 that "we brought nothing into the world, and we can take nothing out of it." Our wealth only has meaning to us in this life. Let us use it to further God's kingdom, and be at peace.

> *The wicked borrows, but his debt*
> *He never does repay;*
> *Whereas the righteous gracious is*
> *And freely gives away.*
> *For those who have been blessed by Him*
> *Inherit shall the land;*
> *And those who have been cursed by Him,*
> *Cut off, shall no more stand.*
> Psalm 37:21–22

A man can do nothing better than to eat and drink and find satisfaction in his work. This too, I see, is from the hand of God, for without him, who can eat or find enjoyment? (2:24–25).

It is at retirement when an individual finds that during his life he has gotten more fun out of his work than out of his fun" (Wallace Stegner). Thus it is that he invents jobs to do. Total unproductiveness does not bring happiness.

A popular pastime is bad-mouthing work. We associate it with discomfort, imprisonment, fatigue, boredom, indignity, and exploitation. We say we are "chained to our desk all day" or "just a cog in the wheel." But we really don't dislike our work as much as we say we do, for work is what we build our lives around. Of course, we like the money we earn from employment, but almost as valuable is the companionship of our fellow workers and the satisfaction of a shared responsibility.

We belong to a crew or a staff or a pool. Jointly we share the triumph of meeting our quota. Together, also, we rejoice at weddings and births. We chip in for flowers when there is a death. Once I shared a hospital room with a woman who was foreman in a box factory. All week long "the girls" came in, bringing news of work and a peculiar jocularity about the double mastectomy that proved to be wonderfully therapeutic. My roommate missed her job and was eager to return. And she could hardly wait to get back on the company bowling team.

A common stereotype puts work and pleasure at opposite ends of the scale. Yet we all have experienced work that was pleasurable, and pleasure which was work. "I've got to rest up from my vacation" is not always a joke! "How was your trip?" we are asked as we take the dustcover off our typewriter. "Fabulous!" we answer, "but it's good to be back."

Work has been called "the scaffolding of life." Comes retirement and we are dangling from a window ledge, sixty stories above the ground. Psalm 94:18 says, "When I said, 'My foot is slipping,' your love, O LORD, supported me." We can trust God to help us through this work transition. When we are on firm footing, He will be ready with something useful for us to do.

> You water the hills with rain from Your sky,
> With fruit of Your works the earth satisfy.
> To nourish the cattle You cause grass to grow;
> For creatures who serve man the plants You bestow.
>
> So man brings forth food by working the earth;
> And wine that he grows his heart fills with mirth;
> To make his face shine he extracts fragrant oil
> And finds bread that strengthens his heart for his toil.
>
> Psalm 104:13–15

There is a time for everything, and a season for every activity under heaven (3:1).

The family was meeting to decide the Big Question: What are we going to do with mother? She simply couldn't manage the big house anymore. And all that lawn to mow!

Claire and Howard had three children and three bedrooms: They couldn't take mother. Bonnie had an apartment: She couldn't take mother. Jim and Karen could manage her for a while, but not all the time: Karen and mother didn't get along too well. Let's see ... there is the church retirement home. Or how about everyone going in together and buying a bungalow in Florida? The warm weather would help mother's arthritis.

Mother, of course, knew the time had come. The house *was* too big for one person. It was almost impossible to find anyone to mow the lawn or clean the windows. She was lonely. Somebody to eat dinner with would be nice. She hated to bother the children every time she needed to go shopping. A place closer to the mall would be handy. Or maybe she should put her savings into a life-care center.

Life has its seasons, "Oh, it's a long, long time from May to December. But the days grow short, when we reach September," the song says. There is an age for caring for preschoolers, as any exhausted grandmother will tell you after a morning of babysitting. There is an age for jamming every minute with activity and hardly feeling winded. There is an age for slower, more reflective work. We do not have to apologize for the season we are in, nor fear it. The autumn of life is as productive as the spring, although results of the work may not be as obvious.

A missionary wrote to his supporters, informing them that his mother had died. During the last years of her life she had risen at four o'clock every morning and prayed for her son and his family. "Who will take her place?" he asked.

Who was old enough to have the time to pray?

Moving out of the family home is not the end of productivity. It is simply an acknowledgment that another season has passed. We can no longer rake leaves, but while the snow falls, we can sit by the fire and pray.

For I have been sustained by Thee
Through birth and early days;
Brought from my mother's womb by Thee,
I'll give Thee constant praise.

Do not reject me in the time
When old age I shall see;
And in my days of failing strength
Do not abandon me.

But I with lasting confidence
Will hope continually,
And I will add still more and more
To all the praise of Thee.

Psalm 71: 6, 9, 14

...A time to be born and a time to die, a time to plant and a time to uproot, a time to kill and a time to heal, a time to tear down and a time to build ... (3:2–3).

A survey of people over sixty revealed that few of them feared death. They felt that they had seen and done a lot in their half-century plus ten and were willing to die if that should be the case. Tempered with willingness was inevitability, a condition the young are protected from by a society that promises eternal youth. Eat this vitamin or apply this face cream, the ads say, and take twenty years off your life. Keen agers know better.

We can view the inexorable passage of time from the perspective of a slave or an employee. Either we are helpless victims ruled by a cruel taskmaster, or privileged workers given a precious commodity to use so productively that we and others will greatly prosper. God gives us the choice. "Be very careful, then, how you live—not as unwise but as wise, making the most of every opportunity, because the days are evil" (Eph. 5:15–16). The King James Version uses the expression "redeeming the time." We can compare time to a book for trading stamps, which, when completely filled, can be exchanged for merchandise of equal value.

God is much more generous than department stores. He promises us far more than what we turn in!

However we use our time, it must come to an end. There is in this fact a definite blessing. Life is limited. We will not keep on getting older, and older, and older, enduring a never-ending process of debilitation. How gracious of God to plan a time for us to die! He does not keep his children forever separated from His presence, but one day takes us home to heaven where "He will wipe every tear from their eyes. There will be no more death or mourning or crying or pain, for the old order of things has passed away" (Rev. 21:4).

27

For our frame He well remembers;
That we are but dust He knows;
As for man, like grass he rises;
As the flower in field he grows.

Over it the wind now passes;
In a moment it is gone;
In the place where once it flourished
It shall never more be known.

But Jehovah's loving kindness
Unto them that fear His name
From eternity abideth
To eternity the same.

Psalm 103:14–17

... A time to weep and a time to laugh, a time to mourn and a time to dance ... (3:4).

Weeping and mourning are so intrinsically woven into life's experiences, we don't need to be told there is a time for them. Laughing and dancing seem harder to justify. The most dismal sermon I ever heard was preached by a man who believed it was wrong for Christians to play or tell jokes on each other. It brought to mind all the ingenious pranks—to no one's harm—that had been perpetrated on me and my friends over the years. They had been used by the Lord to ease a bad time or point to a human foible. How poor we would have been without them! I thank God for the funny greeting cards, cartoons, and humorous news items that improved my perspective just when I was thinking too much about myself.

The evening of my father's funeral, my brother and his wife, my mother, and my husband and I sat around the dinner table and remembered all the funny things that had happened to my brother and me when we were growing up. How we laughed! After years of concern over my father's failing health and his constant need for care, faithfully provided by mother, it was so good to know that his pain and her labor were over. We had mourned, and would mourn again as we experienced the reality of his going, but that night it was a time to laugh.

Old people can lose their sense of humor. They become so grouchy, no one wants them around. Nothing anyone does can make them smile. Or they express perpetual sadness, so mournful over a lost loved one, that they can't enjoy anything in the present. A widow of seven years was courted by a fine Christian man with whom she was totally compatible. He asked her to marry him. Her daughter urged her to accept: their final years of life would be so much happier if they spent them together. The widow refused, because she thought "daddy would mind."

Have you laughed lately? Maybe you're opposed to dancing, even if it's square or aerobic, but you can laugh. Jesus says in Luke 6 that we are going to laugh in God's hereafter kingdom. We are going to rejoice and leap for joy. Why wait until then?

> *O hear me now, Jehovah!*
> *Be gracious unto me!*
> *To You I cry, Jehovah!*
> *O now my helper be!*
>
> *You now have turned my sorrow*
> *To dancing full of joy;*
> *You loosened all my sack-cloth*
> *And girded me with joy*
>
> *To You sing psalms, my glory,*
> *And never silent be!*
> *O LORD my God, I'll thank You*
> *Through all eternity.*
>
> Psalm 30:10–12

... A time to scatter stones and a time to gather them ...
(3:5a).

Community Church was in the throes of conflict over how the worship service should be conducted. Some of the younger members wanted more spontaneity, more contemporary music. The older people liked the format that had always been used. To keep peace in the congregation, the elders voted to have one contemporary and one traditional service each week. They felt the time had come to break down the rigidity that had characterized Community for fifteen years.

When two young families in the church proposed a change in the church's doctrinal statement, the elders stood firm. Community's stronghold was the Word of God. If it was broken down, there would be constant fighting between groups that had no standard of belief. Peace depended upon the church's traditional adherence to the Scriptures.

Relationships in a church can often degenerate into a battle between the "young turks" and the "old-timers." One group wants to change everything; the other group wants to change nothing. The line between cultural practice and scriptural injunction becomes hazy. Which stone wall guards us from heresy, and which stone wall shields us from innovation?

An excellent guide for handling church conflicts can be found in Acts 15: (1) The settlement was based upon the word of God; (2) cultural differences were taken into account; (3) those more mature in the faith were sensitive to the younger Christians and did not want to burden them with anything beyond some basic requirements; (4) the purpose was to encourage and strengthen their fellow believers.

Those of us who have been in the church a long time

31

might copy this guide on a piece of paper and write across the top: RULES FOR SCATTERING AND GATHERING STONES.

> *Behold how good a thing it is,*
> *And how becoming well,*
> *When those that brethren are delight*
> *In unity to dwell.*
>
> *For it is like the precious oil*
> *Poured out on Aaron's head,*
> *That, going down upon his beard,*
> *Upon his garments spread.*
>
> *Like Hermon's dew upon the hills*
> *Of Zion that descends,*
> *The LORD commands His blessing there,*
> *Ev'n life that never ends.*
>
> Psalm 133

... A time to embrace and a time to refrain ... (3:5b).

Diane and Ruby had been friends since college. They were bridesmaids in each other's weddings. Even when Diane had moved across the country, the two women kept in touch by telephone. Letters and gifts were exchanged. Every five years, when their college class had a reunion, Diane and Ruby would room together and sit up all night talking.

When Ruby was forty-eight, her husband was transferred to the city where Diane lived. Of course, they were invited to stay with Diane and her husband until the moving van came. Diane watched by the window until the car pulled into the driveway. With a cry of delight, she rushed out the front door and greeted Ruby with a hug that lifted her right off her feet. How good it was to be together again!

For her fiftieth birthday, Diane's husband took her to dinner at a restaurant out in the country. As they were making their way to their table, whom should they see but Ruby, with a man they didn't know. Awkward hellos were exchanged. Ruby's introduction of Jim Haskins as her "business associate" did not satisfy Diane, whose birthday celebration was ruined.

The next day Ruby stopped by to explain. She and Jim had been dating for about a month. They both still loved their own spouses, but had found something special in each other. "Now, Diane, don't look so shocked," Ruby said. "This is a new age, remember? It's O.K. to have more than one relationship."

Diane didn't think so. She was terribly hurt and disappointed. This time being a friend meant speaking her disapproval and urging Ruby to confess her sin, repent, and give up Jim. But Ruby wasn't sorry, so Diane sent her away without a hug "for old-time's sake."

Of mercy and of justice,
O LORD, I'll sing to Thee.
In uprightness and wisdom
Shall my behavior be.
O when in lovingkindness
Wilt Thou to me come near?
I'll walk within my dwelling
With heart and life sincere.

I will permit no base thing
Before my eyes to be.
I hate unfaithful doing;
It shall not cleave to me.
The man whose heart is forward
Shall from my presence go;
And nothing that is evil
Will I consent to know.

Psalm 101:1–4

... A time to search and a time to give up ... (3:6a).

The story is told of a man who was walking down the street one day when he spied a dollar bill in the gutter. He spent the next twenty years of his life walking with his head down, hoping for a similar piece of good fortune. He missed seeing the trees bud in the spring, the geese flying south, the sun set. His back grew so humped he couldn't lift his head. He saw a lot of gutters, but he never again found a dollar bill.

Life is marked by occasional surprises—small but bright blessings that give us an unexpected lift. We would like to go back and live them over again, but we cannot. Time has wrought changes. The picturesque park where we realized how much we were in love is now shabby and neglected, a gathering place for drunks. The tour we took on our second honeymoon has been discontinued.

Memory is capricious. Over the years we have magnified the good things and minimized the unpleasant. When we go back to our hometown to see the house where we grew up, we realize the yard is much smaller than we remembered. We had forgotten how noisy the street was.

We can spend the last decades of our life searching for a duplicate of some earlier experience. We can even contrive people and events to fit a bygone mold. We load our children with guilt if they don't keep Christmas the way we did forty years ago. We resist our minister's attempt to change the worship service. If we could only recapture those particular moments when life was so intensely sweet!

There is a time to give up searching. What is lost is lost. We must be alert for the delights that today will bring. If we try a new vacation, a new order of worship, even a new Christmas, we may sense an exhilaration we haven't felt in years.

"Forget the former things; do not dwell on the past. See, I

am doing a new thing! Now it springs up; do you not per-
ceive it? I am making a way in the desert and streams in the
wasteland" (Isa. 43:18–19).

I to the hills will lift my eyes.
From whence shall come my aid?
My safety cometh from the Lord
Who heav'n and earth has made.

Thy foot He'll not let slide, nor will
He slumber that thee keeps.
Lo, He that keepeth Israel,
He slumbers not nor sleeps.

The Lord *thee keeps; the* Lord *thy shade*
On thy right hand doth stay;
The moon by night thee shall not smite,
Nor yet the sun by day.

The Lord *shall keep thee from all ill;*
He shall preserve thy soul.
The Lord *as thou shalt go and come*
Forever keeps thee whole.

Psalm 121

... A time to keep and a time to throw away ... (3:6b).

If you have a Captain Marvel comic book in your basement, don't toss it into the trash. It can be worth at least $255! Mickey Mouse watches, Barbie dolls, and baseball cards bring fantastic prices. Collectibles are big business.

Much that we keep stored in boxes is not valuable to anyone but us. Ticket stubs, blackened corsages, graduation programs are worthless. So is children's artwork. Who wants a drawer full of family photographs? Yet we keep collecting, preserving memories of important occasions.

There are happy memories and sad ones. Perhaps some bitter ones. We remember angry words and hurt feelings. The relative who didn't come to our wedding. The daughter-in-law who told us to stop interfering. The neighbor who never paid back $75 he borrowed in 1963. We keep these in our mental storage boxes, getting them out from time to time and reliving the experience.

In Isaiah 43:25 God says to His people, "I, even I, am he who blots out your transgressions, for my own sake, and remembers your sins no more." All those terrible things we have done—God cancels them, wipes them out. He doesn't stuff them away in a drawer just in case He wants to drag them out to jog His memory. He obliterates them. He can't remember them any more.

Has anyone sinned against us the way we have sinned against God? No, no one, regardless of how badly we think we were treated. Yet God forgives and forgets. And so should we. Why spend our final years hating? Nothing good can possibly come of it. As we hate we become hateful. People avoid us and we are alone.

As we get older we can get careless about our spiritual housekeeping. Emotional trash can collect. This is a good day to confess it, make amends, and enjoy life free from ugly clutter.

37

What blessedness for him whose guilt has all forgiven been!
When his transgressions pardoned are, and covered is his sin.
O blessed the man 'gainst whom the LORD counts no iniquity,
And in whose spirit there is not deceit or treachery.

When I kept silent, my bones aged; my groaning filled each day,
Your hand oppressed me day and night; my moisture dried away.
Then I to You admitted sin, hid not my guiltiness;
I said, "I will before the LORD transgressions now confess."

Then You did all my sin forgive and take my guilt away.
For this when You are near at hand let all the godly pray.
The rising floods will harm him not. You are my hiding place.
And you will comfort me with songs of victory and grace.

Psalm 32:1–7

...A time to tear and a time to mend ... (3:7a).

When Jacob heard the story that his son Joseph had been killed, he tore his clothes, put on sackcloth, and mourned many days. David tore his clothes when he heard of Saul's death; he wept and fasted until evening. The ancients had a proper outlet for their grief.

Our culture is much more restrictive. A widow writes: "... I have learned that grief cannot be denied. No matter how determined we are to throw our shoulders back, and hold our heads high, sorrow takes its toll. At times we feel that we are making progress, and we are proud of ourselves for being brave. Then wham! Along comes some little thing that reminds us of our loss ... a little thing like a song, a phrase, a something that seems to be of no significance reminds us.... We realize that this partner who has shared our life is no longer with us" (Rachel Keels in *Home Life*, November 1980).

Holding our head high when we want to tear our clothes is one of the hardest things to do in life. The words "Try to be brave, dear" help very little. We want to wail and lament, put on sackcloth and ashes, and show our hurt to the world. But we cannot. We are told to buy a new dress— "Something in a bright color"—and to plunge into a sea of activities "to get our mind off our loss."

Those who have studied death and dying agree that a time of grief is essential and therapeutic. Honest acknowledgment of our feelings helps us to face life again without our loved one. But the time comes when tearing must stop. We must begin mending our lives. God offers all His resources. With David we can say, "You turned my wailing into dancing; you removed my sackcloth and clothed me with joy, that my heart may sing to you and not be silent. O LORD my God, I will give you thanks forever" (Ps. 30:11–12).

O Lord, I will exalt You,
  For You have lifted me;
My foes You have allowed not
  To glory over me.
O Lord my God, I pleaded
  That You might heal and save;
Lord, You from death have ransomed
  And kept me from the grave.

His saints, O praise Jehovah
  And thank His holy name.
His anger lasts a moment,
  His grace a whole life time.
For sorrow, like a pilgrim,
  May tarry all the night,
But then a shout of joy comes
  When dawns the morning light.

                    Psalm 30:1–5

... A time to be silent and a time to speak ... (3:7b).

Marion was visiting her son and his family in Colorado. She had a pleasant room with a view of the mountains. Rob had bought tickets for a concert under the stars. Christine went to special trouble to cook delicious low-sodium meals. But what should have been a perfect visit was marred by the tension that existed between Christine and her sixteen-year-old son, Tom. She disapproved of the way he dressed and told him so. She criticized him constantly, and Tom went out of his way to be the irritant she expected.

Marion had been through the same experience with Rob's brother, David. She had received valuable help from a Sunday school class on parenting adolescents. Should she talk to Christine? Would she be considered helpful, or an interfering mother-in-law? She saw so much of David in Tom! Perhaps she should approach Tom first.

Being an older and wiser person creates a dilemma. The Bible condemns meddling and commends counsel. We read in Titus 2 that older women are to train the younger women. James 1:19 says, "Be quick to listen, slow to speak and slow to become angry." Proverbs 19:20 directs us to "listen to advice and accept instruction." What should Marion do?

Here are some questions to ask in your situation: Does my life show that I have taken my own advice? Is my relationship with the other person loving enough that I have the right to speak? Are my motives beyond reproach? Can I bear the other person's response without being hurt or defensive?

If the answers are Yes, then it is time to speak. Not indirectly by hints or innuendos, not sarcastically, but face-to-face in love, giving the counsel the seriousness it deserves.

Because I trust in Thee, O cause Thou me to hear
Thy lovingkindness free, when morning doth appear.
Make me to know the way wherein my path should be,
Because my soul each day do I lift up to Thee.

O LORD, deliver me from all who me oppose.
To Thee alone I flee to hide me from my foes.
No God have I but Thee; teach me to do Thy will;
Thy Spirit's good; lead me on even pathway still.

Psalm 143:8–10

... A time to love and a time to hate ... (3:8a).

Christianity is marked, above all else, by love. How can there be a time to hate? Psalm 97:10 says, "Let those who love the LORD hate evil, for he guards the lives of his faithful ones." David declares in Psalm 101:3, "The deeds of faithless men I hate; they will not cling to me." In Psalm 119:14 the psalmist hates "every wrong path." David asks the question in Psalm 139:21, "Do I not hate those who hate you, O LORD, and abhor those who rise up against you?"

We who love the Lord are to hate sin. Indeed, the Christian life is a battle against it. That's why we are equipped to be soldiers (Eph. 6). Sometimes the veterans get tired and decide to leave warfare to the young recruits. Fighting for truth and justice is wearying. Even being a prayer warrior is less than exciting.

Moses was past eighty when he led the Israelites out of Egypt. The next forty years were full of fighting. Moses got weary. In Psalm 90:13–14 he writes, "Relent, O LORD! How long will it be? Have compassion on your servants. Satisfy us in the morning with your unfailing love, that we may sing for joy and be glad all our days."

At 120 Moses was still warning the people about sin. Just before he died he called them to repentance. In Hebrews 11, the great chapter of faith, it says, "He regarded disgrace for the sake of Christ as of greater value than the treasures of Egypt, because he was looking ahead to his reward" (v. 26). Looking ahead. Anticipating the day when he would be with the Lord.

When we feel like quitting—retiring or even going AWOL—let us remember Moses and look ahead. When we have fought the last battle, God stands ready to welcome us to eternal peace.

Hate evil, all who love the Lord;
He keeps His saints secure,
And from the hand of wicked men
He gives deliv'rance sure.

For all the righteous light is sown,
And true hearts gladness claim.
Ye righteous, in the Lord *rejoice,*
And thank His holy name.

Psalm 97:10–12

. . . A time for war and a time for peace (3:8b).

Here is another reminder that we should expect fighting. Graciously God promises us that throughout our lives there also will be times of peace. Between the fields of battle lie green pastures.

Peace, however, has to be sought. Psalm 34 tells us it has to be *pursued*. David gives us the steps. First, we admit that we are poor and afflicted, troubled and afraid. We call out to the Lord, "Save us!" God hears our cry and offers us refuge. We see that God is good, able to supply all our needs. David does not minimize God's requirement that we fear Him; He demands our obedience to His law. We are to turn from evil and do good. God does not overlook sin.

Those who love the Lord find Him to be a God of justice, but also mercy. He is close to the broken-hearted. He saves those who are crushed in spirit. Yes, we will have troubles, but the Lord will deliver us from them all. Our faith in the Lord saves us from condemnation. Christ has redeemed us. In this life and forever after, we are safe with Him.

This is true peace. Life has times of war when enemies and persecutions mark our days. God knows our limits and will not give us more war than we can bear (1 Cor. 10:13).

Christian soldiers are given "R & R"—rest and rehabilitation. They also have the assurance that God's eternal peace is theirs, no matter what happens.

> *O come, my sons, give heed to me;*
> *I'll teach Jehovah's fear.*
> *Who longs for life and loves full days*
> *That he may see good here?*
> *Restrain your lips from speaking lies;*
> *Keep back your tongue from ill;*
> *Depart from evil, and do good;*
> *Seek peace; pursue it still.*
>
> Psalm 34:11–14

45

He has made everything beautiful in its time. He has also set eternity in the hearts of men; yet they cannot fathom what God has done from beginning to end (3:11).

Robbie looked at the steady downpour and was sorry the cub scout picnic had to be canceled. Grandpa checked the rain gauge with obvious satisfaction: this kind of drenching was just what the summer crops needed. One advantage of age is improved perspective. Short-term gratifications can be traded in for long-term gains.

The fact that the earth is spinning according to plan undergirds the concept that life has a purpose. The orbits of the stars, the seasons, the patterned birth and death of every living creature—all attest to a God of order and design. Nothing in this world is useless or ugly. The armadillo and the duckbill platypus both have a place in God's ecology. No doubt they are also beautiful to other armadillos and duckbill platypuses.

Unlike animals, human beings have both a sense of history and a vision of the future. We do understand perpetuation. While we cannot fathom God's divine purpose from the creation of the world to the establishment of a new heaven and a new earth, we can grasp life as a continuum.

"Ask the former generations and find out what their fathers learned, for we were born only yesterday and know nothing, and our days on earth are but a shadow," says Bildad in Job 8:8–9. Eternal life rings out through the Scriptures, even as their inspired writers admit that our presence here is as tenuous as a blade of grass. Paul writes, "Now we know that if the earthly tent we live in is destroyed, we have a building from God, an eternal house in heaven, not built by human hands" (2 Cor. 5:1).

To the person of no faith, the inexorable passage of time produces no beauty, only a desperate compulsion to extract from life whatever drops of self-satisfaction one can.

The believer knows that his allotted years have a divine purpose, with a beginning and an end that fits into God's master plan for His entire universe.

> When all our sons in sturdy growth
>   Like plants in vigor spring,
> Our daughters corner-stones that grace
>   The palace of a king;
>
> When to afford all kind of store
>   Our garners shall be filled;
> When our sheep, thousands in our fields,
>   Ten thousands more shall yield;
>
> When strong our oxen are for work;
>   When not a foe is nigh,
> Nor is there going forth to war,
>   Within our streets no cry;
>
> The people dwell in happiness
>   Who are in such a case;
> Who take the LORD to be their God,
>   They are a blessed race.

Psalm 144:12–15

I know that there is nothing better for men than to be happy and do good while they live. That every man may eat and drink, and find satisfaction in all his toil—this is the gift of God (3:12–13).

Being happy, eating, and drinking are O.K. with God! In fact, the Spirit-inspired writer says they are His gift! Lest we cast aside our diets and our doctor's advice for a spree of gluttony, we have to accept two contingencies.

First, we see that being happy is related to doing good. Our feeling of well-being comes from giving our best to the task before us. Second, we note that satisfaction is found in toil. We are not supposed to give up working in order to sit around all day, watch TV, and eat doughnuts. The retired person can readily appreciate the blessing of toil, paid for or volunteered. Idleness can be miserable.

Over this picture of happiness a shadow is cast. "While they live" reminds us that death will come. The secularist says, "Eat, drink, and be merry, for tomorrow you die." She disguises her despair in riotous living. The Christian says, "So whether you eat or drink or whatever you do, do it all for the glory of God" (1 Cor. 10:31). Express your assurance of eternal life in such common activities as these.

God's plan for us includes happiness. The enjoyment of an evening spent at a concert, sitting with a sick neighbor, or taking care of the grandchildren reminds us again that our life is part of a far grander program which will culminate, someday, in everlasting joy at the throne of our Creator and Sustainer.

With all my heart my thanks I'll bring,
Before the gods Thy praises sing;
I'll worship in Thy holy place
And praise Thy name for truth and grace;

For Thou above Thy name adored
Hast magnified Thy faithful word.
The day I called Thy help appeared;
With inward strength my soul was cheered.

All kings of earth shall thanks accord
When they have heard Thy words, O Lord;
Jehovah's ways they'll celebrate;
The glory of the Lord is great.

Psalm 138:1–5

*I know that everything God does will endure forever; nothing
can be added to it and nothing taken from it. God does it, so
men will revere him (3:14).*

In an age of planned obsolescence, it's encouraging to
know that everything God does will endure. While we are
coping with the broken toaster-oven we got last
Christmas, and debating whether to trade in the car or
pay another whopping bill for repairs, God is working
with men and mountains. The plan He established even
before the earth was created continues on schedule without factory recall.

John was allowed to understand the great sweep of history when the angel of the Lord spoke to him on the island
of Patmos. The great apostle saw the new heaven and the
new earth and heard Jesus say, "I am the Alpha and the
Omega, the First and the Last, the Beginning and the End"
(Rev. 22:12).

We do not have the prophetic vision of John, but as believers in a sovereign God we are given the mind to appreciate some measure of His eternal plan. Furthermore,
God allows us to share in it, not as inanimate cogs in a
wheel, but as living beings whose nostrils breathe life from
God Himself. Our allotted portion of life is part of the vast
span bridging the alpha and the omega. We may be
infinitesimal, but we are essential.

The unchangeableness of God evokes my praise. God is
dependable. Hallelujah! When the plumbing stops up, and
the boy doesn't come to mow the grass, I am reminded of
life's uncertainties. Just keeping everything going right is
frustrating and exhausting. Then I remember James 1:17:
"Every good and perfect gift is from above, coming down
from the Father of heavenly lights, who does not change
like shifting shadows." Drawing from God's endurance, I
can cope.

Hallelujah! Praise Jehovah!
  O my soul, Jehovah praise!
While I live I'll praise Jehovah,
  Praise my God through all my days.
Put no confidence in princes,
  Nor for help on man depend;
He shall die, to dust returning,
  And his purposes shall end.

Happy is the man who chooses
  Jacob's God to be his aid;
He is blessed whose hope of blessing
  On the LORD *his God is stayed.*
He has made the earth and heaven,
  Seas, and all that they contain;
He will keep His truth forever,
  Rights of those oppressed maintain.

Psalm 146:1–7

Whatever is has already been, and what will be has been before; and God will call the past into account (3:15).

History repeats itself" is a phrase that goes back at least to Plutarch and his fellow Grecians. Economics and politics have a way of going in cycles—or is it circles? Repetition occurs just as often in the microcosmic history of our individual worlds. The latest thing in vegetable gardens is raising the soil one to two feet above the ground—something the French have been doing for centuries. Nor is there anything unique in human relations. The accounts of family turmoil that fill the newspapers all have their counterparts in another time and place.

Koheleth, however, writes this verse from God's point of view, not man's. He reminds us of God's foreknowledge— knowing a thing before it exists or happens. Isaiah repeats God's description of Himself as He says, "I am God, and there is no other; I am God, and there is none like me. I make known the end from the beginning, from ancient times, what is still to come. I say: My purpose will stand, and I will do all that I please" (46:9–10).

God knew that we were going to be here. Our parents may have been surprised at our conception, but God was not! God knows who we are now, down to the very number of hairs on our head. God will remember that we were here; our names are written in His book of life.

There is great comfort in realizing that we are important to God. The Bible verse we learned as little children, "He cares for you" (1 Peter 5:7), means we are not merely a historical statistic, but an object of God's loving concern. With all the billions of people coming and going through time, God can account for us. Personally.

The next time someone comes up to you with a wonderful "new" invention that you saw your grandmother use, think of this, and rejoice.

He made the nations' counsel vain;
The plots the heathen would maintain
Jehovah caused to fail.
Jehovah's counsel shall endure;
His purposes of heart most sure
Through ages all prevail.

The LORD looks forth from heaven high;
On sons of men He turns His eye.
There seated on His throne
He looks to earth on all mankind.
As one He fashions every mind;
To Him their deeds are known.

Psalm 33:10–11, 13–15

53

And I saw something else under the sun: In the place of judgment—wickedness was there, in the place of justice—wickedness was there. I thought in my heart, "God will bring to judgment both the righteous and the wicked, for there will be a time for every activity, a time for every deed" (3:16–17).

A widow living on Social Security in a small house in the city never ventures beyond her front porch. Three times she was mugged on the street. Once her groceries were stolen as she came out of the supermarket. Now she depends on a nearby mission to do her shopping.

Another widow is constantly harassed by a gang of boys who throw garbage on her front lawn and sit on her steps and smoke pot while their radios blare rock music in deafening volume. She has called the police, but as soon as they arrive, the boys disappear. The police cannot patrol her block constantly, and they privately regard her as a nuisance.

"Liberty and justice for all" is not a reality. Many people have neither the strength, tenacity, nor money to fight the wickedness that curtails their personal liberty. Since wickedness also exists in the place of judgment—the court system itself is not immune to corruption—the affects of crime run the gamut from frustration to annoyance to sheer terror and eventual physical assault. Older people are especially vulnerable.

All of this does not go unnoticed by God. He promises that the righteous and the wicked will be brought to judgment. Whatever may go amiss in the legal process down here, we are all going to have our day in God's court. Like Job, we may cry out, "Why does the Almighty not set times for judgment? Why must those who know him look in vain for such days?" (24:1). God answers through David. "The Lord is known by his justice; the wicked are ensnared by the work of their hands. The wicked return to the grave, all

the nations that forget God. But the needy will not always
be forgotten, nor the hope of the afflicted ever perish" (Ps.
9:16–18).

Our timing for retribution may not agree with God's, but
we have the assurance that "there will be a time." Meanwhile we can find patience and strength in prayer, both for
ourselves and those with the responsibility to protect us.

> *Sing praise to the* Lord, *who in Zion does dwell;*
> *Among all the peoples His great doings tell.*
> *When blood He avenges, His memory is clear;*
> *The cry of the poor never fades from His ear.*
>
> Lord, *see what I suffer from malice and hate;*
> *Have mercy! O lift me away from death's gate,*
> *That I with the daughter of Zion may voice*
> *Your praises, and in Your salvation rejoice.*
>
> Psalm 9:11–14

I also thought, "As for men, God tests them so that they may see that they are like the animals. Man's fate is like that of the animals; the same fate awaits them both: As one dies, so dies the other. All have the same breath; man has no advantage over the animal. Everything is meaningless" (3:18–19).

Ken agreed to be a substitute teacher for the junior class in Sunday school, but found himself unprepared for their boisterous activity. Soon the room was full of paper airplanes and spitballs. A game of "boys tease the girls" resulted in chairs toppling over. One girl did a tap dance on the table. "They behaved like a bunch of animals," Ken declared with disgust. There would be no more Sunday school teaching for *him*!

Likening people to animals is most derogatory, but we have to admit that there are similarities. Without the constraint of the Holy Spirit, we too would display bestiality, clawing our way to survival. The capacity for the wickedness cited in verses 16 and 17 of this chapter resides in us all. Even Christians can do terrible things, as the Bible honestly testifies in the lives of individual saints and the nation Israel.

The temptations to do evil that come our way are tests to show us that we *are* like animals. Our baser nature delights in the satisfactions of the flesh. Do we not use the animals to describe our self-indulgence? We "wolf down" food, drink "like fish," live "like pigs," are sly as a fox and deceive like a snake in the grass. We call people we don't like "dogs." Sexual license has an animal vocabulary all its own.

Sad to say, many people want to remain animals. "But man, despite his riches, does not endure; he is like the beasts that perish. This is the fate of those who trust in themselves, and of their followers, who approve their sayings. Like sheep they are destined for the grave, and death will feed on them," says the composer of Psalm 49:12–14. That is the fate of those who look to themselves. Everything becomes meaningless. Those who trust in God will have their souls redeemed from the grave; they will be taken by God to be with Him (Ps. 49:15).

Life and death have purpose when we belong to God.

> *My strength He weakened in the way;*
> *My days He shortened. Then I pled,*
> *"In midlife take me not away,*
> *O God, Whose years will never end,*
> *But will through ages all extend."*
>
> *Of old You earth's foundation laid;*
> *Your mighty hands the heavens made;*
> *Yet they will die, while You endure.*
> *Like garments they will worn our be;*
> *Like clothes You change them constantly.*
>
> *These shall be changed and pass away;*
> *But You are evermore the same,*
> *Because Your years will never end.*
> *Your servants' children dwell secure*
> *Before You, reestablished sure.*
>
> Psalm 102:23–28

So I saw that there is nothing better for a man than to enjoy his work, because that is his lot. For who can bring him to see what will happen after him? (3:22).

Tom never liked his job with the trucking company. Even though the pay was good, the hours were terrible, keeping him away from home nights and weekends. Mr. Valenti was not easy to work for, and his son, who ran the office, wasn't any better. When business slacked off, and Tom was offered an early retirement, it seemed a blessing. Now he could finish paneling the basement. He wanted to put in some dwarf fruit trees and repave the driveway.

With every day free for home projects, the work went amazingly fast. A month after retirement, Tom had nothing to do. He found himself dropping in at the trucking company during lunch hours just to talk with the men. When Dave Roskowski had an operation, Mr. Valenti asked Tom if he could come back temporarily. He jumped at the chance!

It was great to be behind the wheel again. When his CB picked up "Oklahoma Joe" heading north for Minneapolis, he asked him to pull off the road for lunch at the Dixie Diner. The two men had been friends for years, meeting on the highway as they carried freight from one city to another. Yes sir, those had been good times!

"So how's retirement?" Joe asked, squirting ketchup on his hamburger.

"O.K."

"Just O.K.?"

"Well, with Maisie still working, it's pretty quiet around the house all day. Not much to do. I go down to the garage to see the guys a couple of times a week."

"Any chance you might go back?"

"No. Mr. Valenti's grandson is coming on next month when he finishes school. For a long time it looked like he was going into insurance, but he's changed his mind."

"Like father, like son."

"Yea. He'll take up any slack in the payroll. If I had known he was getting into the business, I would have played my cards differently."

"How so?"

Tom mopped up his beef gravy with a piece of bread. "Well, I would have taken that job in billing when they offered it. Young Valenti's going to start as a trucker—the way his grandfather started. I'm the trucker being replaced. I'd be safe in billing, at least for a couple of years."

"Don't blame yourself. We're not fortunetellers."

"That's for sure! We never know how things are going to turn out."

Blessed the man that fears Jehovah
And that walketh in His ways:
Thou shalt eat of thy hands' labor
And be prospered all thy days.
Like a vine with fruit abounding
In thy house thy wife is found,
And like olive plants thy children,
Compassing thy table round.

Lo, on him that fears Jehovah
Shall this blessedness attend;
For Jehovah out of Zion
Shall to thee His blessing send.
Thou shalt see Jerus'lem prosper
All thy days till life shall cease;
Thou shalt see thy children's children,
Unto Israel be peace.

Psalm 128

Again I looked and saw all the oppression that was taking place under the sun: I saw the tears of the oppressed—and they have no comforter; power was on the side of their oppressors—and they have no comforter (4:1).

It is 586 B.C. and Jerusalem has fallen. The Babylonian armies have leveled the protective wall around the city and burned the temple and the palaces. The destruction is complete. Nebuchadnezzar is satisfied.

Out of this setting comes Lamentations, a political funeral song picturing Jerusalem as a former queen who is now a widow-slave. "Bitterly she weeps at night, tears are upon her cheeks. Among all her lovers there is none to comfort her. All her friends have betrayed her; they have become her enemies" (1:2).

Jerusalem was oppressed. She had no comforter. Five times in the first chapter of her elegy she laments this condition. "My groans are many and my heart is faint" (1:22). Her suffering is described: buildings leveled, God's abandonment of His sanctuary, leaders exiled, starvation to the point where mothers eat their own children, death in the streets. As the suffering continues, Jerusalem's enemies respond with applause and sarcasm.

God's people have sinned repeatedly in spite of compassioned warnings by the prophet Jeremiah. This punishment was well-deserved after God's patience became exhausted. But God's justice is never isolated from His mercy. Out of this most degrading circumstance, with Jerusalem experiencing her greatest suffering and oppression, comes one of the most beautiful testimonies to God's steadfast love: "Because of the LORD's great love we are not consumed, for his compassions never fail. They are new every morning; great is your faithfulness" (3:22–23).

In 2 Corinthians 7:10 Paul writes, "Godly sorrow brings repentance that leads to salvation and leaves no regret, but worldly sorrow brings death." When we are truly sorry for our sin, God always forgives and comforts. "For he does not willingly bring affliction to the children of men" (Lam. 3:33).

It is never too late to be sorry. Have you nurtured a sin for decades—adultery, greed, alcoholism, profanity, an unloving attitude? You and your loved ones are suffering. Do you excuse it by saying you are too old to change? This is Satan's deception. God welcomes the repentant sinner at any age.

> *Has God forgotten all His grace?*
> *Has His compassion gone?*
> *Or can it be His mercies all*
> *He has in wrath withdrawn?*
>
> *Then I replied, "Such questions show*
> *My own infirmity.*
> *The firm right hand of Him Most High*
> *Through years must changeless be."*
>
> *The LORD's deeds I remember will,*
> *Thy works of old recall.*
> *I'll ponder all which Thou has done*
> *And weigh Thy wonders all.*
> Psalm 77:9–12

And I declared that the dead, who had already died, are happier than the living, who are still alive. But better than both is he who has not yet been, who has not seen the evil that is done under the sun (4:2–3).

Two statements characterize the speech of people over fifty. One is "I'm glad _____ didn't live to see this day." This could refer to the founder of a business that has gone bankrupt, or the publisher of a magazine that becomes risqué in order to increase subscriptions. We say it about the mother of a child who acts against family principles.

The other statement is "I'd hate to be bringing children up in these times." This reflects on society's lenient attitude toward morality, the influence of television, lack of discipline in the schools, prevalence of drugs, or the high cost of a college education.

The older we get, the more we like to fantasize about "the good old days" (which historians reveal to be not all that good). As my daughter puts it, "You walked to school through the blinding snow, six miles uphill *both* ways!" Either we dream of the past or feel smug that we don't have to wrestle with the future, which we are sure is going to be awful. Meanwhile the present continues, with all its miseries unredressed.

Each week our newspaper carries a list of volunteers needed to work in social agencies. In the church, too, there is a never-ending need for people to visit, teach, cook, and care-for. Titus 2 calls upon older women to train younger women in the fundamentals of marriage and child-rearing. Older people have a specific responsibility to counsel. Paul directs elders to "encourage others by sound doctrine and refute those who oppose it" (Titus 1:9).

Add to social agencies and church the need for workers in political campaigns. Average American Voter is feeling a resurgence of interest in government. Elected officials are becoming more sensitive to the people back home. Christians are banding together to speak out for various moral causes. The 15 percent of our population aged sixty-five and over is another potent force.

Speaking of force, those of us who are compelled to sit quietly at home because of physical limitations have the time and patience to pray ... "to him who is able to do immeasurably more than all we ask or imagine, according to his power that is at work within us" (Eph. 3:20).

There is so much we can do to change today!

Lord, Thou hast searched me; Thou hast known
My rising and my sitting down;
And from afar Thou knowest well
The very thoughts that in me dwell.

Thou knowest all the ways I plan,
My path and lying down dost scan;
For in my tongue no word can be,
But, lo, O Lord, 'tis known to Thee.

Psalm 139:1–4

And I saw that all labor and all achievement spring from man's envy of his neighbor. This too is meaningless, a chasing after the wind (4:4).

We had enough trouble keeping up with the Joneses when they lived next door. Now they are on television, daily urging us to buy a laundry soap or a car just like theirs. We see the "good life"—eating out, looking sexy, playing games, riding a horse through mountain meadows—and we want a piece of the action. "You can be forever young and sensual," the ads say. We look at our aging bodies and envy those who appear to make it all true.

Does *all* labor and achievement spring from envy of our neighbor? *All*? Unless it is done for the glory of God, it does. Either we desire things to glorify ourselves or to glorify Him. There is no middle motivation. The person separated from God can fool herself with all kinds of altruistic reasons for achieving in the marketplace, but even generosity with possessions can ultimately be prompted by the hope of self-exaltation.

What is the value of achievement anyway? We can only enjoy accolades and acquisition for a short time, and then we die and leave them behind. We may leave them behind before that, if we are too old to make use of them. Scrambling to get to the top in meaningless, a chasing after the wind. David captures the essence of this futility when he says, "Man is a mere phantom as he goes to and fro: He bustles about, but only in vain; he heaps up wealth, not knowing who will get it. . . . Each man's life is but a breath" (Ps. 39:6, 5).

Ecclesiastes does not encourage sloth. God does want us to be industrious. Knowing how much work is enough is a complex matter. The Teacher has more to say.

Behind, before me, Thou dost stand
And lay on me Thy mighty hand;
Such knowledge is for me too strange
And high beyond my utmost range.

Where shall I from Thy Spirit flee,
Or from Thy presence hidden be?
In heav'n Thou art, if there I fly,
In death's abode, if there I lie.

Psalm 139:5–8

The fool folds his hands and ruins himself. Better one hand-ful with tranquillity than two handfuls with toil and chasing after the wind (4:5-6).

The Hebrew used in verses 5 and 6 is softened by the English translation. The idle fool who refuses to work literally "eats his own flesh." He uses up what little he already has and then must consume himself.

Laziness has its price. God commands us to be industrious, establishing in His Word the rule that "If a man will not work, he shall not eat" (2 Thess. 3:10). Proverbs enjoins us to till the land and harvest the crop. "Do not love sleep or you will grow poor; stay awake and you will have food to spare" (20:13).

There has to be a balance, of course. The Bible doesn't say become a workaholic to the neglect of everything else. It doesn't say stay awake so long you get sick. Rather, work to meet your needs. Work to help other people meet their needs. When working destroys your tranquillity (freedom from disturbing emotions), slow down.

Paul understood this concept. He writes to Timothy, "But godliness with contentment is great gain. For we brought nothing into the world, and we can take nothing out of it" (1 Tim. 6:6). A handful of house and yard that we can enjoy is far better than two handfuls with all the extra care that they entail. We can't take it with us anyway, so wherever we live, let's keep it reasonable.

> *If I the wings of morning take*
> *And utmost sea my dwelling make,*
> *Ev'n there Thy hand shall guide my way,*
> *And Thy right hand shall be my stay.*
>
> *If I say, "Darkness covers me,"*
> *The darkness hideth not from Thee.*

To Thee both night and day are bright;
The darkness shineth as the light.

My inward parts were formed by Thee;
Thou, e'er my birth, didst cover me;
And I Thy praises will proclaim,
For strange and wondrous is my frame.

Psalm 139:9–14a

Two are better than one, because they have a good return for their work (4:9).

A test to determine your "medical age," in which a low score is desirable, gives a plus-six to the person living alone at or after age forty. The score is based on life insurance statistics which reveal that living alone is a stress situation that shortens life.

The Bible recognizes this fact in its very first chapters. God said, "It is not good for the man to be alone. I will make a helper suitable for him" (Gen. 2:18). We see companionship exemplified in Ruth and Naomi, Jonathan and David. Jesus sent his first ministers forth "two by two." One lamb among many wolves would have no protection.

The principle of mutual helpfulness is most beautifully demonstrated in the concept of the church as a *body* of believers. Christians are "joined and held together by every supporting ligament" for the purpose of growing and building each other up in love, "as each part does its work" (Eph. 4:16). One Bible commentator goes so far as to note that in the body itself there are pairs—two legs, two ears, two hands, etc.

I was working at the Sunday school table one Sunday morning when a woman came in the back door of our church building. I greeted her and asked the usual questions as to her name and what had brought her to our church. "I'm lonely and looking for friends," she replied quite honestly. She was a widow who had lived in Brazil for twenty-five years, and she had just moved to be near her oldest daughter. I assured her that in our church she would find many friends, which has proved to be true.

Our visitor had begun her quest for friends in the right way. She admitted her need and then went to the place where friends can be found. So often we suffer from loneliness, hating to admit our need for friends, as if that were

68

something to be ashamed of. The Bible teaches that the need to belong was placed in us at the Creation. It is natural and healthy. We are not to hide ourselves in the house, never venturing forth where people are.

Nor are we to fantasize that someone else is going to take responsibility for us and whisk us away for a day of scintillating adventure. Reality decrees that we must leave our shelter to find a suitable companion. Only Eve was created out of a rib. We must make the first move, and the best place is to the house of God's people. There we can find friends ready to welcome us.

> How lovely, LORD of hosts, to me
> The tabernacles of Thy grace!
> O how I long, yes, faint to see
> Jehovah's courts, His dwelling place!
> My heart and flesh with joy draw nigh
> As to the living God I cry.
>
> Blest they who in Thy house abide;
> To Thee they ever render praise.
> Blest they who in Thy strength confide.
> And in whose heart are pilgrims' ways.
> They make the vale of tears a spring,
> With showers of blessings covering.
>
> Psalm 84:1–2, 4–6

If one falls down, his friend can help him up. But pity the man who falls and has no one to help him up! (4:10).

A friend assists us. We may fall down literally on an icy sidewalk, or fall down figuratively on the job. Our friend picks us up, dusts us off, and gets us started again.

A close friend may keep us from falling. "Do you really think you should do that?" she asks, her voice loving but concerned. She acts as a second conscience. I am about to speak harshly at the teachers' meeting, when I wonder, "What will Mary Anne say?" Or "That movie is off-color. Would Evelyn go?" A friend prays that we will not stumble: she holds us up before the Lord, as a person in need of direction. A friend restores us: her balm might be words of encouragement of a jar of homemade chutney; she has confidence we will walk again, and she lets us know it.

I was leading a retreat on the subject of friendship when a woman asked if she could speak to me privately. She "confessed" that her husband was her best friend and she wondered if that was all right. I was happy to reassure her. Surely the oneness of marriage is not only a physical union, but a compatibility of minds and spirits as well. The definitive passage on marriage in Ephesians 5 describes the relationship as one in which each person helps the other to be more like Christ. This is exactly the goal of friendship.

DeWitt Wallace, who founded *Reader's Digest*, was bitterly discouraged at the early rejections of his unique idea. Then he met and married Lila Beth Acheson, who was sold on his conception of a periodical comprising short, distilled articles. She worked and sacrificed with DeWitt. Eventually the Wallaces found themselves heading a publishing phenomenon. One senior editor said, "They have been mutually supportive to the nth degree. He needed a woman who believed in what he was doing, and I'd guess that they talked about manuscripts almost every evening of their married life." Wallace himself said, "I think Lila made the *Digest* possible."

The word given in the Bible for building up another person's faith is "edification." In Romans 14:19 Paul enjoins us to "make every effort to do what leads to peace and to mutual edification." Friends use their friendship to do this.

> *I'll hear what God the LORD will speak,*
> *Ev'n peace to those His face that seek,*
> *And to His saints, if only they*
> *No more in folly's path will stray.*
>
> *Together met are truth and grace,*
> *While righteousness and peace embrace;*
> *Truth, springing forth, the earth doth crown,*
> *And righteousness from heav'n looks down.*
>
> *Before Him righteousness shall go,*
> *And in His steps our pathway show.*
> Psalm 85:8, 10–11, 13

Better a poor but wise youth than an old but foolish king who no longer knows how to take warning. The youth may have come from prison to the kingship, or he may have been born in poverty within his kingdom (4:13–14).

It is always hard to admit that we're too old for the job. We feel like the person we were twenty years ago. The work is getting done. We don't realize that others are compensating. Our assistant is remembering things we forget, but not letting us know. The management process has been quietly rearranged so that we are bypassed.

We can get too old for the job at church too. We follow our fixed routine, unaware that times have changed. A church treasurer was terribly hurt when the finance committee hired a computerized accounting service. For a quarter of a century the man had practiced a ritual of counting the offering on Sunday. As the church had grown, it had taken him longer, but he really enjoyed it. Now that important part of his life was gone.

We also get settled in our religious views. We like our particular interpretation of the Bible. When the new minister preaches on a subject close to our spiritual nerves, we wince from the pain. What does he know anyway? Some upstart fresh from seminary! "Why, he got in a lot of trouble when he was a teen-ager. Said so himself! Wasn't saved until he was twenty-two. I've been a Christian all my life!"

Age is not a barrier to Christian service. Rigidity is. A woman eighty years old has just arrived in South America for a two-year term of service as a missionary assistant. She must have decided that whatever she was doing at home could be done better by someone younger. No doubt she has a teachable spirit and a flexible temperament, or she would never be accepted to serve in foreign missions!

Are you movable and teachable?

Thou art my hiding place; Thou shalt
From trouble keep me free;
With songs of my deliverance
Shalt Thou encompass me.

I will instruct thee and thee teach
The way that thou shalt go;
And with Mine eye upon thee set
I will direction show.

Then be not like the horse or mule
Which do not understand;
Whose mouth, that they may come to thee,
A bridle must command.

                                   Psalm 32:7–9

Guard your steps when you go to the house of God. Go near to listen rather than to offer the sacrifice of fools, who do not know that they do wrong (5:1).

How casually we approach worship! We arrive at church hardly prepared for an hour in the immediate presence of God. We are still digesting our breakfast, Saturday night's TV show, and the argument we had in the car on the way over. When we finally get settled in the pew we are again tempted to forget all about God. We are either upset because the flower arrangement is askew, or so relaxed we fall asleep. Wasn't that a sharp elbow we just felt in our left rib cage?

Some of the sharpest words Jesus ever spoke had to do with the way people worship. He had absolutely no patience with hypocrisy. In Matthew 23 He condemns those who call attention to themselves by the way they dress, and those who take the most important seats in church. He comes down hard on the legalists, scrupulously counting the leaves in their herb plants so that one-tenth of them goes into the temple treasury, but neglecting justice, mercy, and faithfulness. With scathing words He calls for repentance. We are not to come out of a worship service unchanged.

Jesus grieved that the Jerusalem worshipers had no regard for their prophets. In every one of his letters, Paul commends those who preach the Scriptures. The writer of Hebrews tells us that we are to combine hearing the gospel with obedient faith (4:2). When we go to church we are to *listen.* God wants attendance with attention.

To listen we must come prepared to hear. This requires discipline long before we greet the usher outside the sanctuary door. Note that we are to guard our steps when we *go to* the house of God, not just when we get inside. Be ready to meet with God. Watch your step!

Truly Thou art not a God
   That in sin doth take delight;
Evil shall not dwell with Thee
   Nor the proud stand in Thy sight.
Evil doers Thou dost hate;
   Liars Thou wilt bring to naught.
God abhors the man who loves
   Deed of blood or lying thought.
But in Thine abundant grace
   To Thy house will I repair;
Looking to Thy holy place,
   In Thy fear I'll worship there.

Psalm 5:4–7

> *Do not be quick with your mouth, do not be hasty in your heart to utter anything before God. God is in heaven and you are on earth, so let your words be few. As a dream comes when there are many cares, so the speech of a fool when there are many words (5:2–3).*

My daughter talks in her sleep—long, complicated sentences. If you listen closely, you can tell what she is thinking in her dreams. She just can't put her mind to rest!

The writer of Ecclesiastes is emphasizing the point that when we worship, we are to listen. Prayers should be thoughtfully spoken. That our words be few does not necessarily refer to length. Solomon's prayer of dedication of the temple was very long. Jesus prayed all night. Rather what matters is content. Jesus tells us not to "keep on babbling like pagans, for they think they will be heard because of their many words" (Matt. 6:7). Have you ever sat in a prayer meeting and wondered if the person praying out loud had fallen asleep and was rambling like a dreamer? Have you ever found yourself doing that in your personal devotions? You wake with a start to hear yourself saying the same thing over and over!

Scripture here marks a definite distance between God and man. The holy writers did not picture God as "the man upstairs." Their conception of God can be summed up in the Westminster Shorter Catechism: "God is a Spirit, infinite, eternal, and unchangeable, in his being, wisdom, power, holiness, justice, goodness, and truth," Such a God is to be worshiped "acceptably with reverence and awe" (Heb. 12:28).

If we are struck speechless when we first meet an important person, how much more should we be slow to speak before Jehovah, "I am who I am"!

O come and to Jehovah sing;
  Let us our voices raise;
In joyful songs let us the Rock
  Of our salvation praise.
Before His presence let us come
  With praise and thankful voice;
Let us sing psalms to Him with grace;
  With shouts let us rejoice.

The LORD's a mighty God and King;
  Above all gods He is.
The depths of earth are in His hand;
  The mountain peaks are His.

O come and let us worship Him;
  Let us with one accord.
In presence of our Maker kneel,
  And bow before the LORD.

                              Psalm 95:1–4, 6

77

When you make a vow to God, do not delay in fulfilling it. He has no pleasure in fools; fulfill your vow. It is better not to vow than to make a vow and not fulfill it. Do not let your mouth lead you into sin. And do not protest to the temple messenger, "My vow was a mistake." Why should God be angry at what you say and destroy the work of your hands? (5:4–6).

When Ed went into the hospital for heart surgery, the doctor told him it would be touch and go. Ed called his lawyer and made sure his will was in order. He phoned Will Haskins at the bank and arranged for him to be the executor of his estate. He explained to a tearful Mary what she was to do if he died.

The morning of the operation, Ed lay in bed thinking about life. He had taken it for granted up to now. It suddenly hit him that he didn't want to die. Sixty-two wasn't old: he could put twenty more years to good use. "God," he said, "if you bring me through this ordeal and let me live, I'll start going to church. I'll read the Bible. I'll pray every day." He was actually glad when the hospital chaplain stopped by to offer some words of comfort. "I sure hope God keeps His promises," Ed said to himself as the anesthesia began to take effect.

The earliest mention of a vow in the Bible is Genesis 28:20, where Jacob promised to set up the place he was at as a sanctuary, if God would bring him safely to his father's house. Like all vows, it sprang from his consciousness of his entire dependence on the will of God and the obligation to be thankful. Such a vow was a serious matter. "It is a trap for a man to dedicate something rashly and only later to consider his vows," says Proverbs 20:25. Better not to promise anything at all than to let a vow go unfulfilled. We can't go to our minister and say, "I made a vow to God under stress, but now that I'm O.K., I don't want to keep it. Can I buy the church fifty new hymnals instead?"

Does God have a right to be angry about this kind of wheeling and dealing? Yes, because He takes promises seriously—His and ours. He may destroy "the work of our hands," what we have loved and labored to achieve, if we speak without sincerity. Jephthah found this to be true and lost his only child (Judg. 11:29ff.).

In times of crisis, particularly during sickness or affliction, we tend to bargain for blessings. Keeping oaths made in this context should be regarded as mandatory. God doesn't play games.

> *Make your vows to Jehovah;*
> *Pay your God what is His own.*
> *All men, bring your gifts before Him;*
> *Fear is due to Him alone;*
> *He brings low the pride of princes;*
> *Kings shall tremble at His frown.*
> **Psalm 76:11–12**

Much dreaming and many words are meaningless. There-
fore stand in awe of God (5:7).

Daydreams," says Derek Kidner, "reduce worship to verbal doodling." We are in the context of worship again, with
its high demands on our attention. We can put on a hypo-
critical front or pray insincerely or make rash promises to
God. Or we can just sit there and let our minds wander all
over the place. "Shall I ask Mr. Whitcomb for a raise? Would
Dick like a sleeping bag for Christmas? Where is Elizabeth
today—did she and Ted break up? Someone should tell
the custodian to dust under the organ bench."

There are also the daydreams of great things we would
like to do. These fantasies put us on ocean cruisers or
executive boards of large corporations. We see ourselves
thinner, more attractive, younger. We think about ourselves, not God. This is the vanity—the meaninglessness—against which Ecclesiastes is protesting.

"Stand in awe of God." Our response to Him is not stated
more concisely than it is in Deuteronomy 10:12: "And now,
O Israel, what does the Lord your God ask of you but to fear
the Lord your God, to walk in all his ways, to love him, to
serve the Lord your God with all your heart and with all
your soul, and to observe the Lord's commands and decrees that I am giving you today for your own good?" Awe
of God is good for *us*. Think of that!

Going to church is often thought of as a burdensome
duty. And sometimes it is. Worshiping God, however, is
never burdensome. "Worship the Lord in the splendor of
his holiness," says David in Psalm 29:2. What is the result?
He gives us strength and peace (29:11). "Delight yourself in
the Lord and he will give you the desire of your heart," we
read in Psalm 37:4. Wherever we read about worship, a
blessing from God follows. As it is in words, so it surely is in
practice.

> *O praise the* L*ORD*! *With all my heart*
> *Thanks to the* L*ORD* *I'll bring,*
> *Where upright ones assembled are*
> *And congregations sing.*
>
> *The works accomplished by the* L*ORD*
> *Are very great in might.*
> *They are sought out by everyone*
> *Who finds in them delight.*
>
> Psalm 111:1–2

As goods increase, so do those who consume them. And what benefit are they to the owner except to feast his eyes on them? (5:11).

While visiting in the eastern United States, I was invited to tour an estate that had been opened to the public. The grounds with their gardens, fountains, and pools were so extensive it took three hours to see them all. The warm spring air had brought out the best in the flowering bulbs and trees. Freshly sprouting shrubbery provided a verdant backdrop for Greek and Roman statuary. The large solarium was filled with exotic plants.

I was glad the owner of the estate had allowed people like me to see it. He and I were alike in that respect: we looked at the same yellow daffodils, the same pink dogwood. He had spent thousands of dollars on his gardens, employing a large staff to maintain them. No doubt they brought him a lot of pleasure, but his visual delight was no greater than mine.

A missionary friend of mine was speaking to a group of women gathered in the living room of a suburban mansion. When the place for the next meeting was announced, the prospective hostess asked to be replaced. Her cleaning service would be unable to come the day prior to the meeting. The more we own, the more help we need to keep it in good repair. As the old saying goes, we are possessed by our possessions.

We read in 1 Kings 4:22ff. of the daily provisions for King Solomon: 185 bushels of fine flour and 375 bushels of meal. That's a lot of bread! Many people were eating at Solomon's expense. No doubt there was a lot of graft, with the head baker slipping a few loaves to his wife's brother-in-law, who sold them in the market and split the difference. How many people were employed to care for Solomon's 12,000 horses? A special staff had to be appointed just to keep track of the barley and straw. Just think of the monumental book-keeping—without computers!

Solomon's wealth attracted thousands of parasites, including 700 wives and 300 concubines. All these women enjoyed Solomon's riches, meanwhile telling him how wonderful he was. He couldn't refuse them anything, even their detestable gods. God had to punish Solomon by taking away his kingdom. After he died, it wasn't his wisdom the people remembered; it was the oppressive taxation caused by his lavish lifestyle.

What benefit are the things you own, to you?

That man is good who graciously
And freely gives and lends,
Who justly governs his affairs,
Who truth and right extends.
There surely is not anything
That ever shall him move;
The righteous man's memorial
Shall everlasting prove.
He has dispersed his wealth abroad
And given to the poor;
His horn with honor shall be raised,
His righteousness endure.
Psalm 112:5–6, 9

The sleep of a laborer is sweet, whether he eats little or much, but the abundance of a rich man permits him no sleep (5:12).

Maybe the rich man is sleepless because he's worrying about whom he's going to appoint as vice-president in charge of marketing, or whether he should buy out Consolidated Condominiums. But verse 12 states that it is his *abundance* that keeps the man awake. Too many helpings of prime rib, asparagus hollandaise, and chocolate mousse! Heartburn makes rest impossible.

The laborer, meanwhile, is snoring away. He didn't have a big supper, but he worked hard all day. His wife told him not to go bowling, but he went anyway, and now he's exhausted. It's 11:30 and he's fast asleep, his bowling ball left in the front hall where somebody's going to trip over it.

How curious is our present obsession with physical fitness! We spend money and effort to undo the damage of too much money and ease. We buy power lawn mowers so we can cut the grass quickly in order to get to the health club. Teen-agers need their own cars to drive to football practice. Our supermarkets have such a plethora of available food, advertised in appealing TV commercials, that it is almost impossible not to overeat. Diet pills and stomach-ache remedies sell in the millions. The No. 1 prescription medication in our country today is Tagament, an ulcer drug introduced in 1977.

But there is nothing wrong with abundance. God promises it! "The Lord will grant you abundant prosperity—in the fruit of your womb, the young of your livestock and the crops of your ground—in the land he swore to your forefathers to give you," Moses says in Deuteronomy 28:11. In the Psalms we find repeated reference to God's abundant provision. He *wants* us to enjoy the good things of the earth.

Can we have abundance and a good night's sleep too? It all hinges on how we use our wealth. God's promises are always contingent upon our obedience to His word. If we use God's gifts to further His kingdom here on earth, we shall be given more. Jesus affirms this in the parable of the talents (Matt. 25).

The years between fifty and sixty are a good time to rethink what we should be doing with our money. The children are grown and self-supporting. We can more easily move into a simpler lifestyle. We have past expenditures to evaluate. What is really worth buying? We have accumulated a lot of knowledge about the needs of the church—diaconal, missionary, evangelistic, hospitable, etc. What should we be supporting?

When our abundance is properly channeled, we can enjoy a good night's rest.

> *Except the LORD shall build the house*
> *The builders lose their pain;*
> *Except the LORD the city keep*
> *The watchmen watch in vain.*
> *'Tis vain for you to rise betimes,*
> *Or late from rest to keep,*
> *To eat the bread of toil; for so*
> *He gives His loved ones sleep.*
> *Lo, children are the LORD'S good gift;*
> *Rich payment are men's sons.*
> *The sons of youth as arrows are*
> *In hands of mighty ones.*
> *Who has his quiver filled with these,*
> *O happy shall he be;*
> *When foes they greet within the gate*
> *They shall from shame be free.*
>
> Psalm 127

I have seen a grievous evil under the sun: wealth hoarded to
the harm of its owner, or wealth lost through some misfor-
tune, so that when he has a son there is nothing left for him
(5:13–14).

The fact that the wealth spoken of in verses 13–14 was lost through some misfortune indicates that it wasn't due to gambling or an illegal activity. The cause was outside the person—perhaps a stock market crash or a fire that leveled the factory. The owner's financial advisor may have given him poor advice. Whatever the reason, all the money is gone and the family is destitute. The rich man or woman toiled and worried, spoiling their lives both in the getting of riches and the losing of them.

We can sound very spiritual at this point and say that no wealth at all is better than wealth traumatically lost. I wonder how many of us believe this? Last spring I spent a night in a luxurious hotel. Our suite had a king-size bed, two color TV sets, and a kitchenette. The swimming pool was surrounded by lush tropical trees. When we got tired of swimming we could sit in the sauna or the whirlpool. We ate our meals in the elegant dining room (while I admired the kitchenette, I had no intention of cooking!), served by a waitress, a waiter, and a man who did nothing but pour water. "This is the life," I said to my pampered self. "If it's true that luxury is bad, I would like to try it for a few months, and see."

The key word in these verses is "hoarded," or kept. The Hebrew implication is that the wealth was guarded; it wasn't shared. This is what harmed the owner. He missed the blessing of giving his money away. He didn't experience the joy of seeing other people made happy by his abundance. One of those people was his own son.

The righteous will behold and fear,
  Will laugh at him and say,
"Behold the man who would not make
  Our God his strength and stay."

"This is the man who placed his trust
  In wealth's abundant store,
And in the evil he desired
  Confirmed himself the more."

But I within the house of God
  Am like an olive tree,
And in the steadfast love of God
  My trust shall ever be.

Forever I will give Thee thanks,
  What Thou hast done proclaim;
In presence of Thy godly ones
  I'll wait on Thy good name.

Psalm 52:6–9

Naked a man comes from his mother's womb, and as he comes, so he departs. He takes nothing from his labor that he can carry in his hand (5:15).

Grandchildren are born without clothes on. In the joy of deciding which parent they look like, this fact is somewhat obscured. Death is not associated with nakedness either. Much attention is given to what the deceased will wear in the coffin. Sometimes a special garment is purchased from the mortician. We talk about how "real" the body looks—how beautiful, how peaceful.

The early Egyptians filled their tombs with all the necessities of an afterlife, including the deceased person's spouse and servants, who were conveniently killed for the purpose! Today we are too enlightened to practice such foolishness. Yet we refuse to face the reality that when we die we will carry nothing in our hands.

Two questions need to be answered: What are we doing with our wealth while we are here? What plans have we made for our wealth after we die? Both questions require spiritual as well as financial insight. The complexities of investments, with their fluctuating interest rates and tax advantages, require professional counseling. Some ways of giving to the Lord's work are more productive than others. Then, of course, there is the whole matter of a will—the one thing we always put off until tomorrow.

Paul wrote to Timothy, "But godliness with contentment is great gain. For we brought nothing into the world, and we can take nothing out of it. But if we have food and clothing, we will be content with that" (1 Tim. 6:6–8). Will we be content with that? What about houses with furniture, automobiles, video cassettes, cross-country skis, and chocolate *Monopoly* sets? They help us to be content too.

We may enjoy them while we are here, but how long that will be we do not know. A man who bought a cabin cruiser died before he ever got to use it. They buried him in his new captain's uniform, but he couldn't sail his boat out of the mortuary. He had to leave his beautiful clothes behind too.

After Job got the news that he had lost his children, servants, sheep, camels, and house, he fell to the ground in worship and cried, "Naked I came from my mother's womb, and naked I will depart. The LORD gave and the LORD has taken away; may the name of the LORD be praised" (Job 1:20). All that we have is a gift from God. When we use it to praise Him, we free ourselves from anxiety. We can depart in peace.

> *Yet evermore I am with Thee:*
> *Thou holdest me by my right hand.*
> *And Thou, ev'n Thou, my guide shalt be;*
> *Thy counsel shall my way command;*
> *And afterward in glory bright*
> *Shall Thou receive me to Thy sight.*
> *For whom have I in heav'n but Thee?*
> *None else on earth I long to know.*
> *My flesh may faint and weary be;*
> *My heart may fail and heavy grow;*
> *With strength doth God my heart restore;*
> *He is my portion evermore.*
>
> Psalm 73:23–26

Moreover, when God gives any man wealth and possessions, and enables him to enjoy them, to accept his lot and be happy in his work—this is a gift of God. He seldom reflects on the days of his life, because God keeps him occupied with gladness of heart (5:19–20).

Isn't it great to know that God isn't against rich people! Here we see that God actually makes some people rich and then tops this off by enabling them to enjoy it! They are so busy using their money for the glory of God, they don't think about getting old.

On the other hand, there are those who work and sweat, worrying about how they are going to get the pleasure that God offers as a gift. All they have to do is seek it in the manner that He has chosen to give it. "How much more will your Father in heaven give good gifts to those who ask him!" Jesus said, immediately relating the promise to the summary of the Law and the Prophets. "In everything, do to others what you would have them do to you" (Matt. 7:11–12).

Doing kind things with our money makes our hearts glad. We have all experienced the excitement of giving someone a gift—seeing her face light up, hearing her cry of delight. Or perhaps she was overwhelmed and cried. Yet we are probably not so aware of the fact that kindness keeps us busy. There are so many needs to be met, we can never be bored. One of the cures for depression is helping another person; we simply don't have time to think about ourselves. And there is the physical activity involved that tires us so we fall asleep as soon as our head hits the pillow.

A retired schoolteacher who volunteered in a city mission was asked how she could go on day after day. "I don't ever have time to think about it," she replied. She had accepted her lot: God wanted her in the mission. She was happy in her work; it was exhilarating to see children learn. Her wealth and possessions, though not monumental, were quite adequate. They did not have to supply all of life's satisfactions. These she found in her work, and she was grateful.

> I'll sing to the LORD as long as I live,
> Sing praise to my God while life He will give.
> My thoughts about Him will sweet pleasure afford.
> For I am rejoicing each day in the LORD.
>
> Consumed from the earth let sinners then be;
> The wicked in life no more let us see.
> And now, O my soul, blessing give to the LORD.
> Let glad hallelujahs ring; O praise the LORD!
>
> Psalm 104:33–35

God gives a man wealth, possessions and honor, so that he lacks nothing his heart desires, but God does not enable him to enjoy them, and a stranger enjoys them instead. This is meaningless, a grievous evil (6:2).

Our writer, Koheleth, makes it clear that in this verse he has a particular person in mind. The situation does not occur for everyone. All of us know people—including non-Christians—who have everything their hearts desire and enjoy it very much. Not every rich atheist dies in agony over the fate of her soul.

But it is true that people can be well-off, have excellent reputations, and be miserable inside. Their emptiness may not be apparent. The social milieu of the wealthy affords a sophisticated screen which allows them to "put on a good show." One common cover-up is the enormous debt carried by caterers and florists who serve those living beyond their means. These kinds of businesses are in the dilemma of needing the money, but fearful that too much pressure will alienate the customer who may, eventually, pay the bill.

We can differentiate here between enjoyment from self-gratification and enjoyment from seeing others made happy by our sharing what God has given us. Selfishness does not produce the ultimate satisfaction, although the selfish will dispute this. The key lies in understanding that God's grace, which calls us to a life of service in the name of Christ, also produces enjoyment. The unsaved person can never understand this without enlightenment from the Holy Spirit.

In keeping with the particular situation Koheleth talks about, it is possible that a stranger may come along and enjoy what the rich person has been spending his life working for, particularly if the wealth has been allowed to accumulate. The stranger may take advantage because of outside catastrophe such as war or natural disaster. It is not uncommon for investors, sensing upheaval in government, to transfer their holdings to Swiss banks. Or life can end abruptly due to accident or terminal disease. The stranger can be the state taking over financial holdings for which there was no will. The saddest example is the person so covetous, so greedy, that he has no loved one to whom he can leave his wealth. After he has died, the relatives will gather, virtual strangers, to dispute the disposition of his estate.

Psalm 39 addresses this person, calling him a "mere phantom," heaping up wealth, not knowing who will get it (v. 6). Jesus talks about him too, in the parable of talents. He did nothing good with his money, so he was thrown out into the darkness, where he wept and gnashed his teeth.

> *"Thou with rebukes dost chasten man for sin;*
> *His beauty fades beneath the touch of death;*
> *It is consumed as by the fretting moth.*
> *Oh, surely every man is but a breath.*
>
> *"Lord, hear my prayers; heed Thou my cry and tears;*
> *A stranger here I pass as all before.*
> *O spare me that I may recover strength*
> *Before I go away and be no more."*
>
> Psalm 39:11–13

A man may have a hundred children and live many years; yet no matter how long he lives, if he cannot enjoy his prosperity and does not receive proper burial, I say that a stillborn child is better off than he (6:3).

Two things had predominant value in the Old Testament economy: many children and a long life. Psalm 128:6 sums up the ultimate blessing when it says, "May you live to see your children's children."

Even with heirs and longevity, we are in a sad state if we cannot enjoy our prosperity, capped off with a decent funeral and all the family gathered around. In fact, we would be better off not having lived at all. Mark Twain sensed the possibility that we may be mixing up our values when he said, "Why is it that we rejoice at a birth and grieve at a funeral? It is because we are not the person involved." At least the stillborn child has not suffered from the misuse of his wealth. He comes without meaning, he departs in darkness, and in darkness his name is shrouded (6:4).

To us beyond middle age, the whole matter of funerals takes on personal importance. We realize that the cost, the location, the ceremony, and the accouterments all reflect the person lying in the coffin. How do we want to be represented? The alternatives range from a wake fueled by ample supplies of whiskey to an evangelistic service with no casket present. We can be cremated or give our body for medical implants. The choice will be the expression of how we use our prosperity. So will the number and kind of people who attend.

The man who fails to enjoy his prosperity because he cannot acknowledge that it belongs to God will not rest comfortably in this life or the next. If his lifespan were two thousand years, it would make no difference to his indifferent heart. When he dies, he will spend eternity in the same place as the unbeliever who is poor. Hell does not have first-class and tourist accommodations.

> *Save me by Your hand, O Lord,*
> *From worldly men of earth,*
> *Who only in this present life*
> *Know anything of worth.*
>
> *But as for me, with righteousness*
> *Shall I behold Your face.*
> *I shall be satisfied to wake*
> *And see You face to face.*
>   Psalm 17:14–15

All man's efforts are for his mouth, yet his appetite is never satisfied (6:7).

The mark of a good diet is filling you up with so many low-calorie foods that you don't feel hungry. Weight control means lots of raw vegetables. But no matter how much chopped lettuce you eat, the stomach will soon send out signals that it is empty. Out comes the salad bowl again.

If the goal of one's life is not to please God, it is reduced to a cycle of working in order to eat for strength to go on working to go on eating. Whether we are speaking of an appetite for food or television or taking group tours to exotic places, there is no ultimate satisfaction. We always need more.

After Jesus fed five thousand people with five small barley loaves and two fish, He took a boat ride across the Sea of Galilee. The crowd found Him there and asked Him, "Rabbi, when did you get here?" Jesus wasn't fooled for one minute into thinking all those people were concerned for His welfare. He knew what they really wanted: another free dinner. "Do not work for food that spoils, but for food that endures to eternal life, which the Son of Man will give you," He told them. The crowd wanted to know what kind of food that was. Manna from heaven? (John 6).

Jesus explained that the only food that endures is He Himself. He is the Bread of Life. They should be hungry for (believe in) Him. He would satisfy their deepest soul's desires so they would never be hungry or thirsty again. In fact, a person who ate the Bread of Life would be so well-fed he would never die.

This was a very hard teaching. It still is. Our physical needs are so apparent we cannot deny them. But our spiritual needs can be avoided. Whenever our soul gets hungry it is easy to think the answer lies in a change of scene or a shopping trip. Indeed, when we are spiritually out of tune, we may try to solve the problem by eating!

A steak with a baked potato is a temporary satisfaction. In six hours we will be hungry again. "Why spend money on what is not bread, and your labor on what does not satisfy? Listen, listen to me, and eat what is good, and your soul will delight in the richest of fare," declares the Lord in Isaiah 55:2. Eat the bread of life—believe in Jesus Christ as Lord and Savior—and you will never be hungry again.

Because Thy grace is more than life
My lips Thee praise shall give;
I in Thy name will lift my hands
And bless Thee while I live.

My soul with rich, abundant food
Shall be well satisfied;
With shouts of joy upon my lips
My mouth shall praise provide.

Psalm 63:3–5

What advantage has a wise man over a fool? What does a poor man gain by knowing how to conduct himself before others? (6:8).

Years ago, *Life* magazine carried an article about our country's most successful party crasher. Pictures showed this man at a socialite's wedding, eating with congressmen at a state dinner, and hobnobbing with the rich and famous at a fancy country club. Affairs that required engraved invitations were no barrier; the party crasher had a presence so convincing, he was admitted without question.

With a little practice and one good suit, anyone can pretend to be somebody important. As long as the evaluation depends upon dress and bearing, the rich and the poor can appear to be the same. There are also situations in which rich people dress to appear poor. Famous personalities plagued by autograph hounds and pestiferous photographers have been known to assume disguises that let them mingle with hoi polloi. Both groups learn that every economic lot has its problems.

The contrast here is not only between the rich and the poor. The Wisdom Literature of which Ecclesiastes is a part uses the term *wise* to describe the person who believes in God. The fool is the one who refuses to acknowledge Him even after repeated instruction. ("The fool says in his heart, 'There is no God'" [Ps. 14:1]). Koheleth would also have us look at the Christian and the non-Christian. Is the former any better off materially? Obviously, from everything we can observe, she is not. There are horribly wicked people rolling in money, and virtuous saints barely existing on Social Security and food stamps. We cannot equate spirituality with prosperity. Sad to say, many Christians have been duped by unrealistic promises made by other Christians who completely disregard the depraved world in which we find ourselves.

We are brought back again to accepting our means as God-given and best for us. We are to use what we have to bring glory to our heavenly father. He who is not fooled by appearances will make the proper assessment of our souls at the appropriate time.

> *The fool in heart is saying,*
> *"There surely is no God."*
> *Corrupt and vile their deeds are;*
> *Not one of them does good.*
> *The LORD looks down from heaven*
> *On sons of men abroad*
> *To see which one has wisdom,*
> *If any seeks for God.*
>
> Psalm 14:1–2

Whatever exists has already been named, and what man is has been known; no man can contend with one who is stronger than he (6:10).

The Hebrew root of the word for "man" means "being taken from the earth." God gave man a name that would forever remind him of his humble origin: he was made from dust.

It would seem preposterous that such a lowly creature as this would contend with God, but it is the practice rather than the exception. Job is the classic example. "I would state my case before him and fill my mouth with arguments. I would find out what he would answer me, and consider what he would say," he cries in 23:4–5. When Job and the Lord finally have their dialogue, God asks, "Will the one who contends with the Almighty correct him? Let him who accuses God answer him!" Job can only respond, "I am unworthy—how can I reply to you?" (40:2, 4).

Before we criticize Job, let us remember that we share his nature. We "talk back to God," Paul writes in Romans 9:20. We are clay telling the potter how we want to be formed. We all want to be Chinese Ming vases instead of pickle crocks.

The idea that man is the center of the universe is the prevailing philosophy in the world today. It is called humanism—"any system ... of thought ... in which human interests, values, and dignity are taken to be of primary importance, as in moral judgments" (*Random House College Dictionary*). In other words, man decides what is right and wrong, what is important. He becomes his own potter.

This error can be found in Christians too. We tend to think of ourselves more highly than we ought to think. Satan appeals to our arrogant nature and tries to convince us that we have arrived at our particular station in life by our own efforts. We talk about the "self-made man," a "single-handed operation," "pulling ourselves up by our own bootstraps," and "coming up the hard way." God's Spirit firmly redirects us to His Word, where we are told that everything we are and have comes from God. "Ascribe to the Lord, O mighty ones, ascribe to the Lord glory and strength," David writes in Psalm 29:1. The Lord is King forever, and our strength comes from Him.

> *O give to Jehovah, you sons of the Mighty,*
> *Both glory and strength to Jehovah accord!*
> *O give to the Lord His name's greatness of glory!*
> *In splendor of holiness worship the Lord!*
>
> *The Lord on His throne sat above the great deluge!*
> *The Lord on His throne sits as King without cease!*
> *The Lord is the One Who gives strength to His people!*
> *The Lord is the One Who will bless them with peace!*
>
> Psalm 29:1–2, 10–11

The more the words, the less the meaning, and how does that profit anyone? (6:11).

More about contesting God's decisions. "But who are you, O man, to talk back to God? 'Shall what is formed say to him who formed it, "Why did you make me like this?"'" (Rom. 9:20). Oh, we may not ask Him out loud, but we grumble a lot about ourselves:

"I have such a large nose, Lord! Even bangs do not help."

"When you made my hips, Lord, were you thinking of a pear?"

"When Moses was 120 years old, his eyes were not weak. I'm half that age and had my glasses changed three times in five years! How can I do needlepoint when I can't see?"

Such verbal wrestling is pointless. Unless we want to spend a fortune on plastic surgery, our faces are what they are. As for the rest of our frames, there is little we can do except keep our weight down and exercise regularly. The only cure for features like big feet is a sense of humor.

God made us very physical. We are sweat glands, intestines, too little hair on our head, too much hair on our legs. As our parts begin to wear down, we become preoccupied with our health. Just ask me how I feel! My answer is complex, involving how I slept last night, my new medicine, the weather, and the pizza my granddaughter insisted I eat. Words, words, all about me. Only those waiting to have their turn stay around to listen. The really interesting conversations are not held in my corner of the room.

Yet, even when I hurt, there are words of encouragement I can give others. Perhaps I can share with someone who has a problem a solution that helped me. I may have to be the one who rounds everyone up for a class on Chinese cooking or a trip to hear a famous speaker. I've been to so many Bible studies, it's time I gathered a few people together and taught them what the Holy Spirit has taught me.

Doctrine, a friend reminded me the other day, is not a collection of cold biblical truths, but a way of life. We express what we believe about God by the things we do. If we believe that God made us, that He knew what is best for us when He did, we will be content with ourselves and use our imperfections to glorify His name. Our preoccupation will be in serving others as we forget ourselves. Even with our arthritis and high blood pressure, our aching feet and fluctuating body temperature, we rejoice in the fact that we are fearfully and wonderfully made.

> O LORD, our Lord, in all the earth
> How excellent Thy name!
> Thou hast Thy glory spread afar
> Upon the starry frame.
>
> O what is man, that Thou dost him
> Within Thy thought retain?
> Or what the son of man, that Thou
> To visit him dost deign?
>
> For Thou a little lower hast
> Him than the angels made;
> A crown of glory and renown
> Hast placed upon his head.
>
> Psalm 8:1, 4–5

A good name is better than fine perfume, and the day of death better than the day of birth. It is better to go to a house of mourning than to go to a house of feasting, for death is the destiny of every man; the living should take this to heart (7:1–2).

Augustus Wellington the Fourth was three days old when he came home from the hospital. His father helped his mother up the steps and seated her in the rocking chair that had been in the family since 1842. Augustus's grandmother and grandfather had seen him in the hospital and remarked at how well he was filling out. His great-grandparents, who had driven over from Friendship Village, were looking at him for the first time.

Great-grandfather Augustus ran his fingers gently over the baby's head. Yes, there was the characteristic bump behind the left ear. He was a Wellington, all right!

Tea and cookies were served while Augustus IV slept in the crib his father and grandfather had used. Great-grandfather helped himself to another chocolate crinkle and then said, "Do you think he'll want to take over the business when he's grown up? These are uncertain days for a hardware store—so much government involvement with payroll deductions, taxes, safety codes, fire regulations. I don't envy the young person starting out today."

His son agreed. "The biggest change is the need for security. We rarely had shoplifting in the forties. Robberies were rare. I can remember being in charge while you went to Rotary Club and feeling perfectly safe, and I was only sixteen! Now we have to have TV monitors and a direct line to the police station."

"Of course, it's always easier looking back," said Great-grandmother Wellington, pouring another cup of tea. "We start out with such high hopes. Only at the other end of life are the facts made plain."

"You're right, mother. I certainly couldn't have foreseen the future when I sold my first bag of nails. But with all these problems, it's been a good business. We're a trusted name in this community. Our money-back guarantee really means something!"

"It would be easy to cheat people," admitted Augustus III. "Some of these novice do-it-yourselfers don't know one grade of lumber from another. They can overbuy too. A man came in the store yesterday and thought he needed a gross of nails to panel a clothes closet!"

There's no substitute for quality and service," stated Great-grandfather, as if he were founding the business all over again. "I went to Ed Palmer's funeral last week. I was moved at how many of the townspeople showed up. Ed wasn't rich, but he sure had a lot of friends because he was so honest in the used-car business."

"We'll teach Augustus the importance of being honest," said his mother, getting up from the rocking chair. "Right now I think the only thing he cares about is his lunch!"

> *The lovingkindness of the Lord*
> *Forever I will sing;*
> *Thy faithfulness to every age*
> *My mouth in song shall bring.*
>
> *"For mercy shall be built," said I,*
> *"Forever to endure;*
> *And in the heav'ns Thy faithfulness*
> *Thou wilt establish sure."*
>
> Psalm 89:1–2

Sorrow is better than laughter, because a sad face is good for the heart. The heart of the wise is in the house of mourning, but the heart of fools is in the house of pleasure (7:3–4).

In Proverbs 15:30 we read that "a cheerful look brings joy to the heart, and good news gives health to the bones." Is Scripture contradicting itself? What is really good for the heart?

Our inspired writer distinguishes between pleasure and joy. The laughter that comes from a "house of pleasure" is like that kind found in a tavern or night club. It is temporary, based on eternal stimulation. This kind of happiness may actually dull the senses and make us forget how temporary life is.

Joy, however, is a fruit of the Holy Spirit, a deep and permanent result of knowing Jesus Christ as Lord and Savior. Death has been faced squarely, acknowledged, and accepted. In explaining His death to His disciples, Jesus said, "I tell you the truth, you will weep and mourn while the world rejoices. You will grieve, but your grief will turn to joy.... Now is your time of grief, but I will see you again and you will rejoice, and no one will take away your joy" (John 16:20, 22).

This kind of joy requires preparation through sorrow. "For our light and momentary troubles are achieving for us an eternal glory that far outweighs them all," Paul writes in 2 Corinthians 4:17. We are going to grieve in this life. We are going to mourn as we encounter sickness and death. We suffer vicariously as our own children work through the trials of marriage and parenthood. These experiences draw us closer to God, the source of strength, the oil of joy.

A wise person is she who acknowledges her need for a savior. The presence of sin all around her makes her

mourn. But Christ's power over sin causes her to rejoice.
Her heart is glad.

> May you sacrifice now sacrifices just,
> In Jehovah only placing all your trust.
> "Who will show us goodness?" many people say;
> The light of Your face, LORD, lift on us, we pray.
> You have given my heart greater joy by far
> Than when grain and new wine most abundant are.
> So in peace I lie down; I will rest and sleep,
> For, O LORD, You only will me safely keep.
>
> Psalm 4:5–8

It is better to heed a wise man's rebuke than to listen to the song of fools. Like the crackling of thorns under the pot, so is the laughter of fools. This too is meaningless (7:5–6).

Sophisticated camping equipment has just about eliminated the need to cook food over an open fire. Those who have tried it know how long it takes to boil a pot of water when you're starting from scratch. First, enough tinder has to be gathered to ignite the larger, long-lasting pieces of wood. Twigs burn easily but furnish little heat. Throw them on the flame and they crackle invitingly, but they will not cook a vegetable soup. It is the quiet, slow-burning logs that do the job.

Advice can be twigs or logs. There is the person who kids us along, making light of our transgression. She does not see the seriousness of our situation, even though we admit it:

"Come on now, everybody skips church once in a while!"

"So you flirted with your neighbor at the Christmas party! That's nothing to get so serious about! Blame it on the holiday spirit!"

When we want to sin, such encouragement is a song—music to our ears.

A wise man's rebuke burns within us like a fire. We cannot easily dismiss his words. "Better is open rebuke than hidden love. The kisses of an enemy may be profuse, but faithful are the wounds of a friend," says Proverbs 27:5–6. We heed the wise man because he loves us enough to speak out. He wounds us, knowing our suffering will be his suffering too. He speaks gently, warmly, perhaps even with a touch of humor, but he does not minimize our sin.

When Nabal refused to give food to David's servants, David took four hundred armed men and set out to slaughter every man in his household. He was stopped by Abigail, Nabal's wife, who reminded him of God's promises of protection and victory. Needless bloodshed motivated by revenge would be an offense forever on David's conscience.

David appreciated Abigail's rebuke. "Praise be to the LORD, the God of Israel, who has sent you today to meet me. May you be blessed for your good judgment and for keeping me from bloodshed this day and from avenging myself with my own hands" (1 Sam. 25:32–33). Quite an admission from a future king, and to a woman besides!

It is not easy to accept a rebuke. Our pride wants us to believe we don't need anyone telling us we have sinned. Yet, through the counsel of wise people—Christians sensitive to the teaching of Scripture—we can be stopped before we sin further. God graciously promises another benefit: we shall be restored to fellowship with other believers. Proverbs 15:31 assures us, "he who listens to a life-giving rebuke will be at home among the wise."

> Let me be smitten by the just;
>   It shall a kindness be;
> It shall be oil upon my head
>   When he reproveth me.
>
> Such oil let not my head refuse;
>   For there shall come the day
> When I in their calamity
>   For them to Thee will pray.
>
> And when their judges by the rocks
>   Are thrown down from their seat,
> Then shall they hearken to my voice
>   Because my words are sweet.
>
> Psalm 141:5–6

Extortion turns a wise man into a fool, and a bribe corrupts the heart (7:7).

As we have said before, a "wise man" in Ecclesiastes refers to a person who believes in God. The fool is he who consistently refuses to acknowledge Him. In this verse we see the power of a bribe. A godly person can be so tempted, he succumbs and forsakes God Himself. Either he was pretending to believe and is now exposed as an impostor, or his fellowship with God has been broken, leaving him guilt-ridden and miserable.

Taking a bribe is such a serious offense that it was included in the Mosaic law first given on Mount Sinai. We read in Exodus 23:8: "Do not accept a bribe, for a bribe blinds those who see and twists the words of the righteous." We look the other way while the payoff is taking place. Truth gets distorted.

She who offers a bribe is as guilty as the one who receives it, of course. Both are motivated by greed—wanting more than a rightful share. The result is a corrupted heart—a heart callous to suffering and deaf to the claims of justice. Ultimately the heart becomes so hardened that dishonesty and injustice become the norm. We on the periphery of government and business expect there to be under-the-table deals and "payola." Naturally the big contractor "takes a little off the top." The public conscience becomes numb to exposés of extortion.

God said through Habakkuk in the sixth century before Christ, "Will not all of them taunt him with ridicule and scorn, saying, 'Woe to him who piles up stolen goods and makes himself wealthy by extortion! How long must this go on?' Will not your debtors suddenly arise? Will they not wake up and make you tremble? Then you will become their victim" (2:6–7). These words are just as true today.

The sons of man are vanity, the best of men a lie;
Together in the balance they are lighter than a sigh.

Then in oppression do not hope; nor yet for plunder lust;
Though power and force may seem to thrive, in this build not your
    trust.

For truly God has spoken once; He twice to me made known;
That strength and power belong to God and unto Him alone;

For so it is that sovereign grace belongs to Thee, my Lord;
For Thou according to his work dost every man reward.

Psalm 62:9–12

The end of a matter is better than its beginning, and patience is better than pride. Do not be quickly provoked in your spirit, for anger resides in the lap of fools (7:8–9).

When you're twenty-five, patience is changing a toddler's training pants. At sixty-five, patience is waiting for a forty-year-old daughter to accept Christ as her Lord and Savior. Only from the vantage point of old age can we see the result of our having to wait. The first baby, the move halfway across the country, the new job, the medical breakthrough, the special friend—all came later than we expected. Now we have an expanded though still incomplete understanding of God's grand design. To quote one of our family maxims: "Hindsight is always 20/20."

These are verses of encouragement. Whatever the trial of faith, never despond. "So this is what the Sovereign Lord says: 'See, I lay a stone in Zion, a tested stone, a precious cornerstone for a sure foundation; the one who trusts will never be dismayed'" (Isa. 28:16). The precious cornerstone is Christ, of greater value than the whole world. In Him are all the promises of God. The person who believes these promises and rests on them with a fixed heart will find peace within the will of God.

Bursts of anger, the response of an impatient spirit, are the mark of a fool. He can wait neither for God nor for other people. He literally sits down with his anger! It settles like a large cat.

As we get older, we can become less patient, using our seniority as an excuse to flail the young. If we wonder whether we are short-tempered, all we have to do is ask someone who knows us well. But there is another kind of anger, less easily detected. It is the quiet seething, the "residing," that prompts us to act unkindly, to retaliate. Some people harbor this anger for years, actually enjoying an excuse to be hateful.

Our pride is the problem. We cannot let go and trust God to work things out. How can we ever find out that the end of a matter is better than its beginning, if we will not let it end?

I waited long upon the LORD,
Yea, patiently drew near;
And He at length inclined to me,
My pleading cry to hear.

He took me from a fearful pit,
From out the miry clay;
He set my feet upon a rock,
Establishing my way.

He put a new song in my mouth,
Our God to magnify;
And many, seeing it, shall fear
And on the LORD *rely.*

O greatly blessed is the man
Who on the LORD *relies;*
Respecting not the proud, nor such
As turn aside to lies.

Psalm 40:1-4

Do not say, "Why were the old days better than these?" For it is not wise to ask such questions (7:10).

The best-selling books in our country today are romantic novels. These paperbacks have an established formula: A beautiful young woman is desired by a good man and an evil man; in the end the good man wins. All this happens in a historical setting in which the greatest problem in life is the rigid custom of courtship established by the wealthy. There is little mention of war, disease, infant mortality, or sewage in the gutters. There is much description of what the hero and heroine wear to suit the prescribed activity of the day. One look at them both on the cover is convincing evidence that they never had to work for a living.

Why do these books sell in the millions? Because people want to think there was a romantic time when nothing seriously wrong ever happened. I can remember visiting a museum with my father and looking at the female mannequins dressed in their elaborately decorated dresses with skirts that brushed the floor. They were so beautiful! Then he told me how dirty the dresses got, how the skirts picked up all the filth of the streets. Washing was a chore, and people and their clothes smelled. An illusion shattered!

We can know former days only by report. Present days are a reality we can feel. In many ways, they *are* better, of course. Cancer and heart disease are not nearly the killers they once were. We are thankful for technological advances in transportation, communication, and the growth and preparation of food. (My father shattered another illusion when he told me that the "bread that mother baked" was often terrible!) In many ways, life is safer, healthier, easier.

Our "old days" may not be as far back as the nineteenth century or as broad as the British Empire. We may bemoan the change in our own neighborhood or the fact that our children don't telephone us every Sunday afternoon anymore. We grumble at the way people in church are too busy to talk with us. The supermarket doesn't deliver. We are unwise, not because we examine the causes and effects of history, but because our spirits are so dissatisfied. We just don't like the way God is doing His job!

We are part of our own problem. What are we doing to be part of the solution to making our present days better? Can we be peacemakers in the family, activists in the neighborhood, sensitive to the needs of others at church, helpful to those who can't get out to shop? Can we write letters to our congressmen and to people of influence in the media? Will our money further a worthy cause?

Peter has some helpful advice in his first letter: "Therefore, prepare your minds for action; be self-controlled; set your hope fully on the grace given you when Jesus Christ is revealed" (1 Peter 1:13). Stop complaining about these new days. Get busy and make them good.

O LORD my God, how many are the wonders Thou hast done!
How many are the gracious thoughts which Thou toward us hast
*   shown!*
No one can sort and set them out; none can compare to Thee!
If I would tell and speak of them, they could not numbered be.

No sacrifice of blood or meal is what Thou has desired;
My ears Thou hast prepared to hear; no off'ring hast required.
Then in response these were my words, "I come! Behold and see!
Within the volume of the book it written is of me:

"To do Thy will I take delight, O Thou my God that art;
Because that holy law of Thine is deep within my heart."
Within the congregation great I righteousness did preach;
Behold, Jehovah, Thou dost know, I'll not restrain my speech.
                                                    Psalm 40:5–9

Wisdom, like an inheritance, is a good thing and benefits those who see the sun. Wisdom is a shelter as money is a shelter, but the advantage of knowledge is this: that wisdom preserves the life of its possessor (7:11–12).

Money shelters, as a way to avoid paying taxes on accrued interest, are a popular investment practice today. Who says the Bible isn't contemporary?

We see again in these verses that there's nothing wrong with having money nor with leaving it as an inheritance. It's good stewardship to have savings and investments, to be able to care for ourselves and not become liabilities to the government or our families. Money is a shelter against dependency.

Money is O.K., but knowledge is much, much better. Knowledge underlies wisdom, and wisdom preserves the life of its possessor. How? Here, as in much of the Bible, "wisdom" refers to the wisdom of salvation. "For whoever finds me [wisdom] finds life and receives favor from the LORD. But whoever fails to find me harms himself; all who hate me love death" (Prov. 8:35–36). "The fear of the Lord—that is wisdom, and to shun evil is understanding" (Job 28:28).

The wisdom that fears the Lord, that evokes the heart to claim Him as Lord and Savior, preserves the lives of its possessors. They are given eternal life. "We know also that the Son of God has come and has given us understanding, so that we may know him who is true. And we are in him who is true—even in his Son Jesus Christ. He is the true God and eternal life" (1 John 5:20).

Money can give us security in this life. As an inheritance it helps those who come after us. The wisdom of salvation secures us now and forever.

The man who fears the Lʏʳʹ *has learned*
The first of wisdom's ways.
They who obey will understand.
Forever lasts His praise.

Psalm 111:10

Consider what God has done: Who can straighten what he has made crooked? When times are good, be happy; but when times are bad, consider: God has made the one as well as the other. Therefore, a man cannot discover anything about his future (7:13–14).

Does God make crooked things? Sometimes it seems that way from our point of view. We find ourselves in the midst of events that are decidedly awkward. Life, with its twists and traps, resembles a miniature golf course.

A mother of four children has a kitchen motto that says, "Lord, give me patience to endure my blessings." Indeed, our good times are as difficult to handle as our calamities! As Jacob prepared for his confrontation with brother Esau, he was so confused he prayed, "I am unworthy of all the kindness and faithfulness you have shown your servant. I had only my staff when I crossed this Jordan, but now I have become two groups" (Gen. 32:10). God's prospering him presented a real problem. How would Esau react to this vast entourage of people and animals?

Ezra found a similar perplexity. He returned to Jerusalem and discovered that there had been much intermarrying of the Israelites with their pagan neighbors. Appalled at this disobedience of God's law, he prayed, "What has happened to us is a result of our evil deeds and our great guilt, and yet, our God, you have punished us less than our sins have deserved and have given us a remnant like this" (Ezra 9:13). God's graciousness was overwhelming.

Our good times and our bad times both come from God. He knows exactly how much of each we can comfortably handle. Both should be accepted as such, without undo analysis about what will happen next. We might find a gift of $200,000 more trouble than our monthly fuel bill.

Here's another kitchen motto to keep it all in perspective: "It is hard to hold a full cup steady."

Food Jehovah gives the hungry,
  Sight Jehovah gives the blind,
Freedom gives He to the pris'ner,
  Cheer to those bowed down in mind.

Well Jehovah loves the righteous,
  To the stranger is a stay,
Helps the fatherless and widow,
  But subverts the sinner's way.

Yea, Jehovah reigns forever;
  Through all ages He is King,
Even He, thy God, O Zion;
  To Jehovah praises sing!
                                    Psalm 146:7b–10

In this meaningless life of mine I have seen both of these: a righteous man perishing in his righteousness, and a wicked man living long in his wickedness (7:15).

To this verse we can all say, "Amen!" It doesn't seem fair that some Christians suffer while non-Christians prosper in everything they put their hands to. A Christian pharmacist who refused to sell sex magazines was denied the franchise to sell all other kinds of magazines. He wouldn't sell cigarettes, so he couldn't sell candy either. Eventually he went bankrupt. The drugstore down the street, with its open display of "girlie" magazines, boomed. It does seem meaningless to run a decent, honest operation. Whoever heard of a liquor store or a massage parlor going out of business?

We can only admit how terribly finite we are and leave the final judgment to God. Our verdict is premature and improperly based. We see only the outside, only the here and now. God sees the inside and the future. "Therefore judge nothing before the appointed time; wait till the Lord comes. He will bring to light what is hidden in darkness and will expose the motives of men's hearts. At that time each will receive his praise from God," Paul tells us in 1 Corinthians 4:5.

There is another consideration. Were our righteousness to be rewarded with material prosperity, we would be good only to be rich. We would equate morality with wealth. We would use this measuring stick on everyone else as well. What havoc this would cause! The poor in particular would be accused of being unrighteous. And aren't they suspected of this already?

God expects us to be righteous for His glory and our good. The final reward must be left up to Him.

O greatly blessed is the man who walketh not astray
In counsel of ungodly men, nor stands in sinners' way,

Nor sitteth in the scorner's chair, but placeth his delight
Upon God's law, and meditates on His law day and night.

He shall be like a tree that grows set by the waterside,
Which in its season yields its fruit, and green its leaves abide;

And all he does shall prosper well. The wicked are not so,
But are like chaff which by the wind is driven to and fro.

In judgment therefore shall not stand such as ungodly are,
Nor in th' assembly of the just shall wicked men appear.

Because the way of godly men is to Jehovah known;
Whereas the way of wicked men shall quite be overthrown.

Psalm 1

Do not be overrighteous, neither be overwise—why destroy yourself? Do not be overwicked, and do not be a fool—why die before your time? It is good to grasp the one and not let go of the other. The man who fears God will avoid all extremes (7:16–18).

Some paraphrasing may be helpful for these puzzling verses. "Do not be self-righteous, neither be wise in your own eyes. . . . Do not be so wicked your heart is hardened."

As we become more knowledgeable of Scripture, there is the danger that we presume ourselves to be more spiritual than those less educated. We feel we have "arrived" in our Christian growth. Soon we move from biblical fact to our own interpretation and expression. We decide that a certain attire is "Christian," or a certain way to worship is according to the New Testament. Younger people, reflecting a different culture, are regarded with suspicion.

Take dancing as an example. When my children were in junior high, I wrote a note to the physical education teacher to ask that they be excused from square-dancing class. Now our church sponsors square-dancing, and teen-agers are invited. Yet nothing has changed in the way we square-dance; indeed, it is a form of recreation resistant to innovation. Moreover, we now see aerobic dance classes combined with morning Bible studies. Some churches are using liturgical dance in their worship. What is scriptural, and what is cultural?

On the other hand, there is a moral cowardice exhibited by some religious people that prompts them to tolerate anything. The attitude of our present society that "a little sin never hurt anybody" goes unchecked. Rather than teach God's Word, these people accommodate. They shrug their shoulders and say, "What can you expect from people today?" As long as they give some acknowledgment of God, they aren't considered too bad. My personal distaste is for entertainers who openly lead lives of debauchery and then sing "Amazing Grace" on TV and in night clubs.

We learn, then, that we can err in two directions: we can deceive ourselves into thinking we are Christians when we really believe in a religious system of our own making, or we can foolishly reject the Christian faith altogether and close our hearts forever to the work of the Holy Spirit.

These extremes can only be avoided by the true wisdom of fearing God. "The fear of the LORD is the beginning of knowledge, but fools despise wisdom and discipline" (Prov. 1:7).

> Thy way teach me, LORD; I will walk in Thy truth;
> Unite my heart Thy name to fear.
> My Lord and My God, with my whole heart I'll praise,
> And ever Thy name will revere.
>
> For great are Thy love and Thy kindness to me.
> My soul from the grave Thou dost raise.
> The proud and the violent seek for my life,
> Forgetful of Thee and Thy praise.
>
> But Thou, Lord, are merciful; gracious Thou art,
> Abundant in truth and in love.
> Turn Thou unto me: Thy rich grace now bestow;
> Thy servant make strong from above.

Psalm 86:11–16

Wisdom makes one wise man more powerful than ten rulers in a city (7:19).

To say, with Hobbes, that knowledge is power is not the same thing as to say, with Koheleth, that wisdom is power. One can know many things and be weak. A brilliant mind is susceptible to corruption.

Wisdom is knowledge of God as learned from His Word. It utilizes knowledge and understanding. Gaining wisdom is a process lasting a lifetime. Like Jesus, we are to grow, or advance, in wisdom. The Greek text compares the experience to making one's way through a forest or jungle. There is a sense of effort, of toil—no quick perusal of a Scripture passage here, but the hard work of serious Bible study.

The power that comes from wisdom prepares the owner for combat. We see the mighty hero pitted against the city fathers, be they politicians or generals or civic leaders. Wisdom is not to be attained for seclusion. It is used to fight the enemy, Satan.

Notice also the ratio. One wise man against ten rulers. That is power!

> *Though parents may betray,*
> *The Lord will care for me.*
> *Teach me, O Lord, Your way;*
> *On level path lead me.*
> *For me my foes in ambush wait;*
> *My way is lined with those who hate.*
>
> *O to my foes' desire*
> *Hand me not over now!*
> *They cunningly conspire*
> *Their charges false to vow.*
> *Their every breath is cruelty;*
> *How hopeless seems my cause to be!*

O had I not believed
That I would surely see
The goodness of the Lord
With those that living be!
Wait for the Lord*! With strength restored,*
Be brave in heart. Wait for the Lord.

Psalm 27:10–13

*There is not a righteous man on earth who does what is right
and never sins (7:20).*

This can be an excuse or a confession. We can throw up
our hands and say, "Well, what do you expect? Nobody's
perfect!" and keep on gossiping or losing our tempers. We
can say, "I'm too old to change," a convenient excuse for
any sinful behavior we especially enjoy.

Or we can confess our sinfulness and acknowledge our
need for the strength of divine wisdom. "I have considered
my ways and have turned my steps to your statutes," writes
the composer of Psalm 119:59. "I have strayed like a lost
sheep. Seek your servant, for I have not forgotten your
commandments" (119:176).

We all sin. We all need wisdom. We never reach an age
when it is safe to be ignorant. Abraham, David, Solomon,
and Peter all had confession to make late in their lives.
Recent studies of senior citizens have revealed the
phenomenon of apathy toward further spiritual growth.
Some of them no longer feel a sense of danger about sin. It
is as if they had a reserve of righteousness on which to
draw so that fresh insights into God's word are no longer
necessary. Accompanying this decline of concern is a
drawing back from attendance at worship services and a
disinterest in the church program.

Sometimes the church is at fault for not recognizing the
particular needs of those over fifty-five. Money goes to the
youth ministry rather than the ministry to senior citizens.
The problem can be solved in two ways: we can ask for
help, and we can help ourselves. "Encourage one another
and build each other up, just as in fact you are doing," Paul
says in 1 Thessalonians 5:11. We are our own best resource.

In his second letter, Peter tells his dear friends to (1) "be
on your guard so that you may not be carried away by the
error of lawless men and fall down from your secure posi-

tion," and (2) "grow in grace and knowledge of our Lord and Savior Jesus Christ" (3:17–18).

Good advice for Christians, whatever their age.

All my iniquities blot out; my sins hide from Thy view;
Create in me a spirit right; O God, my heart renew.
O from Thy presence cast me not, thy face no more to see;
The Holy Spirit utterly take not away from me.

The joy which Thy salvation brings again to me restore;
And with a willing spirit them uphold me evermore.
Then in Thy ways will I instruct those that transgressors be,
And those that sinners are shall then return again to Thee.

Psalm 51:9–13

Do not pay attention to every word people say, or you may hear your servant cursing you—for you know in your heart that many times you yourself have cursed others (7:21–22).

Marcie Miller had always been "touchy," but as she grew older, the problem grew worse. Jo Anne asked her to hang up her coat when she came to Bible study, and she pouted for two days. No one wanted to be on a committee with Marcie. If you asked her to put more mayonnaise in the potato salad, she regarded it as a personal attack on her forty years of culinary experience.

Then she began to generalize. When the Sunday school superintendent gave a lesson on using visual aids, Marcie was sure the whole thing was a set-up to criticize the way she taught the second-grade class. She listened to Reverend Crosby's sermons just to hear when he was talking about her. He might say he wasn't thinking of anyone in particular, but Marcie knew better! No one could convince Marcie that the women's council didn't sit around at its Friday meetings and think of ways to cut her down. When she got to church on Sunday morning and found someone had moved *her* fern in the entry, she was sure of it!

Things came to a climax when Marcie overheard Tina Lewis and Carrie Shears, the high school girl who did her cleaning, talking in the restroom about every woman in the church. Marcie was amazed at how much the girls knew. Their parents must have given them an earful! She had to say something—it wasn't good for young girls to gossip like that.

"Carrie," she said, "I'm sure your parents would be disappointed to hear your conversation. Even if what you say is true, they would want you to keep it confidential."

"Oh, I'm sorry, Mrs. Miller," Carrie responded, her face turning pink. "I didn't know you were listening. All I did was tell Tina all the things I've heard you say when I was working over at your house."

They that for my life are seeking
Snares for me in secret lay,
Hurtful things against me speaking,
Plots devising all the day.

As one deaf and dumb appearing
Naught I hear, nor silence break;
I'm as one their words not hearing,
And whose lips no answer make.

Psalm 38:12–14

129

*I find more bitter than death the woman who is a snare,
whose heart is a trap and whose hands are chains. The man
who pleases God will escape her, but the sinner she will
ensnare (7:26).*

Adultery is a two-way street. There has to be someone
enticeable and someone to do the enticing. Female prosti-
tutes wouldn't be in business long if there were no men
willing to pay for their services.

What kind of woman is a snare? She may be "sexy" in the
TV sense of the word. More likely she is empathetic and
warm, the sort who says, "There, there, dear, I understand
even if your wife doesn't." Another snare is the woman-
who-needs-to-be-counseled. She has long private sessions
with her minister or therapist, developing with him a relationship far deeper than the patient-doctor circumscrip-
tion. Men can be trapped and chained simply by being
close to a woman day after day at work. With half the
women in the United States now employed, this propin-
quity is a natural preclusion to intimacy. Some men see the
women in the office a lot more often than they do their
wives.

Taking into consideration the context of the verse—the
emphasis upon wisdom—we see the woman who is a
snare in a much broader sense. She is spiritual adultery,
the folly and meaninglessness of loving someone other
than Christ. We see her in Proverbs 9, sitting at the door of
her house, "calling out to those who pass by, who go
straight on their way. 'Let all who are simple come in here!
. . . Stolen water is sweet; food eaten in secret is delicious!'"
(vv. 15–17).

Spiritual adultery may be personified in the sexy, show-
biz church with its visceral music and continual "high," or
the cult which says, "There, there, dear, I understand even
if your church doesn't." She may be the critic who engages

130

in long discussions that tear down the Word of God. She may be the nonbeliever who influences the believer simply by being around all the time.

Adultery is alluring. She is subtle. Proverbs says she appeals to those who lack judgment. Ecclesiastes says the person who pleases God will escape her. The best defense is obedience to His word. The sinner—the unrepentant one going his own way—is ensnared. He falls into a trap, entering the house of folly, thinking he will join his friends in having a thrilling time. He doesn't know "that the dead are there, that her guests are in the depths of the grave" (Prov. 9:18).

> The men of double mind I hate;
> Thy law my love has stirred!
> Thou art my shield and hiding place;
> My hope is in Thy word.
>
> Depart, ill-doers, that I may
> My God's commandments heed.
> Sustain as Thou hast promised me
> That I may live indeed.
> Quench not my hope, but hold me safe;
> Thy statutes I'll respect.
> All those whom from Thy statutes err,
> In scorn Thou dost reject.
>
> Psalm 119:113–118

"Look," says the Teacher, "this is what I have discovered: Adding one thing to another to discover the scheme of things—while I was still searching but not finding—I found one upright man among a thousand, but not one upright woman among them all. This only have I found: God made mankind upright, but men have gone in search of many schemes" (7:27–29).

This passage doesn't do much for the cause of women! Not one upright woman among a thousand? Of course, men don't fare too well either. Our writer found only *one* upright man.

The Teacher is speaking here of his own experience. He could be looking at the harem in King Solomon's court and regretting the quality of women he sees. They were pagans, and they turned Solomon's heart after other gods. They persuaded him to build an altar "for Chemosh the detestable god of Moab, and for Molech the detestable god of the Ammonites" (1 Kings 11:7). The wives who worshiped different gods made their demands for altars too, and soon there were mini-temples all around Jerusalem. When Solomon writes in Proverbs about the disastrous affects of adultery, he knows from experience! "I have come to the brink of utter ruin in the midst of the whole assembly" (5:14).

How did all this happen? Koheleth sums it up quite succinctly: "God made man upright, but men have gone in search of many schemes." God made Adam and Eve perfect, but they sinned in the Garden of Eden. Ever since, men and women have tried to satisfy their soul's longings with false religions. "For since the creation of the world God's invisible qualities—his eternal power and divine nature—have been clearly seen, being understood from what has been made, so that men are without excuse. For although they knew God, they neither glorified him as God nor gave thanks to him, but their thinking became futile and their foolish hearts were darkened" (Rom. 1:20–21).

The solution is wisdom as found in the Scriptures. Job knew this: "The fear of the Lord—that is wisdom, and to shun evil is understanding" (28:28). Fear of the Lord leads to sorrow for our sin, repentance, cleansing through the blood of Jesus Christ. By God's grace we are saved from the power of sin. This grace empowers us to say no to ungodliness and worldly passions, and to live self-controlled, upright, and godly lives in this present age (Titus 2:12).

> *With sinners gather not my soul;*
> *Spare me from blood they spill.*
> *In their hand is a wicked scheme;*
> *Their right hand bribes do fill.*
>
> *But as for me, I'll humbly walk*
> *In my integrity.*
> *Redeem Thou me, and in Thy grace*
> *Be merciful to me.*
>
> Psalm 26:9–12

Anyone who is among the living has hope—even a live dog is better off than a dead lion! (9:4).

The director of our city zoo was on the radio today. One of the questions he had to answer came from a woman who is campaigning to close all zoos. She cited one in particular where the animals are kept in cramped, dirty cages with nothing to do but sleep. Instead of being half-dead, they should be free, roaming the meadows and mountains, she felt.

The only lions most of us will ever see are in zoos. Even if the king of beasts lives in a simulated Kenyan grassland, without bars or cages, we cannot fully appreciate his majesty. Take him out of his homeland and something is lost.

Dogs, on the other hand, have gone from the status of a lowly, despicable scavenger to a position somewhat above people. The largest single category of food in our supermarket is for dogs. Canines have their own beauticians, clothiers, doctors, schools, and vacation spas. We hear of a lot more cases of child abuse than of mistreating a dog. A live dog in the United States is pretty well off!

Not so in ancient times. Back then, the lion was the noblest of creatures. Jesus is called "the Lion of the tribe of Judah" in Revelation 5:5. Dogs were at the bottom of the animal ladder. Again in Revelation (22:15), the vilest people are likened to dogs.

Seen in proper context, if one is alive, it is better to be a miserable dog than to be a superb, dead lion. As long as there is the breath of life, there is hope—hope of salvation, hope of righting wrongs, hope of healing relationships, hope of making life happier for someone else.

As long as we are among the living we can be hopeful. From my hospital bed I can pray for the lost, witness to the medical staff, encourage the Christians who come to visit. I am never too old or too sick to make someone else happier. It isn't my status in the animal kingdom that makes the difference, but the basic truth that I am alive—alive in Christ. "For everything that was written in the past was written to teach us, so that through endurance and the encouragement of the Scriptures we might have hope" (Rom. 15:4).

> *I rose ere the dawn of the morning and cried,*
> *My hope by Thy promises stirred.*
> *And ere the night watches were passed I awoke*
> *To meditate still on Thy word.*
>
> *In Thy lovingkindness give ear to my voice;*
> *As promised, O LORD, quicken me.*
> *They come ever closer who evil pursue,*
> *Who stray from Thy law and from Thee.*
>
> *But Thou, O Jehovah, art nigh unto me,*
> *And true is Thine every command.*
> *From Thy testimonies I'm certain Thou hast*
> *Established them ever to stand.*
>
> Psalm 119:147–152

Enjoy life with your wife, whom you love, all the days of this meaningless life that God has given you under the sun—all your meaningless days. For this is your lot in life and in your toilsome labor under the sun (9:9).

We must remember that when the teacher in Ecclesiastes uses the word *meaningless*, he means "empty and purposeless." The theme running through the entire book is that a life without fear of God that prompts obedience and love is exactly that: meaningless. But even when we do fear God, there are times of perplexity when we wonder just what His intentions are. We can believe what happens is for our good and still be unsure of what that good is. My young friend who just had a miscarriage may not know for many years, if ever, why—after two full-term pregnancies—the third ended so abruptly.

Rather than dwell on such puzzling matters, we are told to enjoy life. Certainly there is much toilsome labor under the sun, but there are happy times, too. The Lord gives these to us and then stamps on them a sticker that says, "Smile, God loves you."

Our happiness is further enhanced by a marriage partner. The passage does not direct everyone to take a wife; Scripture supports both marriage and celibacy, depending on individual circumstance. In this case, the point is that, if you are married, love your wife and enjoy life with her. She can, in fact, be the difference—the source of joy—that gives life worth. Peter catches the essence of this teaching when he writes, "Husbands, in the same way be considerate as you live with your wives, and treat them with respect as the weaker partner and as heirs with you of the gracious gift of life, so that nothing will hinder your prayers" (1 Peter 3:7).

We note that the element for enjoying life together is love. Marriage is not to be dependent on an endless round of social activities that keep both participants on an artificial emotional high. The joy comes from the relationship itself, the loving another more than we love our own bodies. Indeed it is during crisis that we can enjoy each other the most. A wife afflicted with cancer commented on the precious times she and her husband had during his visits to the hospital. A couple whose son ran away from home learned how much they needed each other; they found joy in prayer together.

Finally, we see that God wants us to enjoy and to live *all the days* of this life. It is said twice for emphasis. Perhaps two-thirds of your "all" is gone. Seek God's help to make the remaining third truly meaningful.

> *But let all that trust Thy care*
> *Ever glad and joyful be;*
> *Let them joy who love Thy name,*
> *For they guarded are by Thee.*
> *And a blessing rich, O Lord,*
> *To the righteous Thou wilt yield;*
> *Thou wilt compass him about*
> *With Thy favor as a shield.*
> Psalm 5:11–12

Whatever your hand finds to do, do it with all your might, for in the grave, where you are going, there is neither working nor planning nor knowledge nor wisdom (9:10).

Maggie Kuhn, in a dialogue on aging, disagrees with those who call congregations with many older members "dying churches." She regards such churches as "skill banks and reservoirs of rich, untapped, undervalued human resources and stimulating power desperately needed to renew and heal our sick society."

Did you ever think of yourself as a "rich, untapped, undervalued resource"? Well, you are! You have spiritual gifts, talents, experience, wisdom, patience, and time. You have a tested value system and a sense of priority. Job knew this when he said, "Is not wisdom found among the aged? Does not long life bring understanding?" (12:12).

You are desperately needed. There is no dearth of work for your hands to do. "I know," you sigh, "but I'm tired. The thrill is gone." The solution may lie in changing what your hands do. You don't have to teach the same Sunday school class for forty years. You don't have to be the Missions Chairman forever. How about heading a committee to influence legislation for Christian principles? Or working with the diaconate in its ministry to the poor? Does the preschool department need a surrogate grandparent with a comfortable lap?

You sigh again. "I don't have the energy I used to have." God asks us to work with all our might, whatever that amount is. He doesn't expect us to equal someone else's might. If we are capable of two good productive hours a day, these belong to Him. The person with eight hours has her own responsibility.

There is no retirement in Scripture. Jesus said, "As long as it is day, we must do the work of him who sent me. Night is coming, when no one can work" (John 9:4). In the grave there will be no work, but that's the only place where inactivity is permissible. And this leads us to an epitaph on a gravestone: "Here lies Maggie, my beloved wife, under the only stone she ever left unturned."

> *I've kept the pathway of the Lord*
> *And from my God did not depart,*
> *I've kept His judgments in my sight,*
> *His statutes shut not from my heart.*
>
> *Sincere toward Him, I set my guard*
> *To keep myself away from sin.*
> *My righteousness the Lord rewards*
> *As in His sight my hands are clean.*
>
> Psalm 18:21–24

I have seen something else under the sun: The race is not to the swift or the battle to the strong, nor does food come to the wise or wealth to the brilliant or favor to the learned; but time and chance happen to them all (9:11).

Koheleth makes a general observation "under the sun" that requires no spiritual insight. Anyone who observes life at all knows that the winner of a contest is often a surprise. The whole premise of gambling is the element of chance. There is always the "dark horse," the upset, the "come-from-behind winner." Human ability cannot guarantee success. Ask any manager of a professional ball team.

The fool who does not believe in God views life as one big video game with a zap here and a zap there, as the invaders from outer space race across the screen in random patterns. But the believer's life is also characterized by unexpected events. He too has to make steps into the unknown and grapple with events out of the blue. He can be affected by evil times as well as the nonbeliever. When natural calamity strikes, the birds and fish of all theological persuasions are equally trapped.

What makes the difference is the believer's assurance that there is God's providence at work, secret though it may be. "In him we were also chosen, having been predestined according to the plan of him who works out everything in conformity with the purpose of his will, in order that we, who were the first to hope in Christ, might be for the praise of his glory" (Eph. 1:11–12). God is not gambling.

We are not really in charge of our lives. "There is no wisdom, no insight, no plan that can succeed against the LORD" (Prov. 21:30). We may cry out that it is unfair: our abilities should make a difference. Until we face a crisis and we aren't feeling strong or we can't think what to do or we have no money. Then God's control of time and chance is a decided blessing.

140

The LORD upholds the meek and brings the wicked to the ground,
With thanks, O praise the LORD our God; with harps His praises
sound;
Who covereth the heav'ns with clouds, who for the earth below
Prepareth rain, Who maketh grass upon the mountains grow.

He cares for beasts that roam the field and doth their food supply;
He watches o'er the ravens young and feeds them when they cry.

In strength of horse or speed of man the LORD takes no delight;
But those that fear and trust His love are pleasing in His sight.

Psalm 147:6–11

141

The quiet words of the wise are more to be heeded than the shouts of a ruler of fools. Wisdom is better than weapons of war, but one sinner destroys much good (9:17–18).

In the arena of human deliberations, some people win by outshouting everyone else. Others resort to threats or engage in actual combat. The "weapons of war" may not be SSTs or battleships. We can fight with money or the power of our position in the company. The vice-president in charge of payroll has a ballistic advantage over the project engineer who wants a raise.

The quiet words of the wise do not always receive serious attention. Koheleth is not saying that wise words go unheeded because they are spoken quietly. Sometimes wisdom calls out so loudly she can be heard above the noise in the street.

The test of the volume lies in the ear and not the voice. The person listening for wisdom can hear it, no matter how softly it is spoken; she who doesn't want to hear is deaf, no matter how many decibels are used. A mother can shout at her son that his room is messy, but if he is engrossed in watching TV, he won't hear. She can whisper that his girlfriend is coming over to borrow a book, and he will be off in a flash to comb his hair.

We must do more than simply *hear* wise words. *Heed* means "pay close attention to, give serious consideration." We can hear someone talk to us while we are reading the paper, but our occasional "uh-huh" is not heeding. Wisdom requires a response based upon a spirit of receptivity. We are ready to listen, and we intend to do something about what we have heard.

The disposition to be wise comes from the Holy Spirit. Paul prayed for the Ephesians, "I keep asking that the God of our Lord Jesus Christ, the glorious Father, may give you the Spirit of wisdom and revelation, so that you may know him better" (1:17). The disposition to hear words of wisdom from the wise also comes from the Spirit. "It is written in the Prophets: 'They will all be taught by God.' Everyone who listens to the Father and learns from him comes to me" (John 6:45).

We should want to be wise and wiser. The alternative is destruction.

> Jehovah's perfect law restores the soul again;
> His testimony sure gives wisdom unto men;
> The precepts of the LORD are right,
> And fill the heart with great delight.

> The LORD's command is pure, enlightening the eyes;
> Jehovah's fear is clean, more lasting than the skies.
> The judgments of the LORD express
> His truth and perfect righteousness.

> They're more to be desired than stores of finest gold;
> Than honey from the comb more sweetness far they hold.
> With warnings they Thy servant guard;
> In keeping them in great reward.

> Psalm 19:7–11

As dead flies give perfume a bad smell, so a little folly out-weighs wisdom and honor (10:1).

The apothecary selects from his jars of aloes, cassia, cinnamon, myrrh, frankincense, and spikenard a particular blend whose fragrance he finds pleasing. Carefully he boils them together into an extract and mixes this with oil. The mixture is poured into a pot to age. Alas, his apprentice fails to put a lid on the pot. A fly falls in, putrifies, and spoils the entire precious batch. A day's work destroyed by one small fly! (Or one small apprentice.)

It takes far less to ruin something than to create it. A single reckless moment can undo an honorable reputation. Recent history is replete with examples of men in high government positions who lost everything because of a little folly—an affair, getting drunk, collusion, bribery. Not repeated foolishness, but just one indiscretion, and a family and career are ruined.

How did the fly get into the ointment? Was the apothecary to blame for not capping the pot himself? Was he too busy, or did he think he was too important for that job? Was the apprentice irresponsible, or perhaps new and needing closer supervision? Was the shop so cluttered no one could find the lid? Maybe a caravan went down the street and everybody ran outside to watch, forgetting all about the newly made perfume.

How does a little folly become so important it outweighs wisdom and honor? First of all, we *want* to act foolishly. The boss wants to sleep with his secretary. The accountant embezzles because she wants to buy a bigger home. No one—not God, not society, not our friends—forces us to behave dishonorably. We willfully choose to reject wisdom. Proverbs 1 tells us we love our sinful ways, we delight in mockery, we hate knowledge. We ignore advice, we will not accept a rebuke, we laugh at disaster.

Is your life being wrecked by a little folly? Are you blaming it on someone else? It's the fly's fault for falling into the perfume! God calls you to confess your own sin, repent, and be restored. It is His will for us that we be able to discern what is best so that we "may be pure and blameless until the day of Christ" (Phil. 1:10).

> O LORD, to those men who are good
> Show Yourself good and kind,
> And likewise show Your goodness to
> All them of upright mind.
>
> Yet shall the LORD drive out all those
> In crooked ways who dwell,
> Along with all who practice sin;
> But peace on Israel!
>
> Psalm 125:4–5

If a ruler's anger rises against you, do not leave your post; calmness can lay great errors to rest (10:4).

Mrs. Cartwright had always been unbearable, but lately she was impossible. No one could please her, not even Melanie Farrell, whose office procedures were seldom less than perfect. Mrs. Cartwright gave a lecture on the proper attire for secretaries. She threatened to remove the coffee-break center completely if people didn't keep it clean. Melanie got dressed down for wasting paper. Everyone had to stay an extra half-hour the night Anne misplaced the Technich account. The final blow came when Mrs. Cartwright took "Abner," the office dieffenbachia, and dumped him in the trash. "This is not a plant shop," she said. "We don't have time to stand around discussing the health of an overgrown tree!"

Charlotte and Anne quit. Melanie went home in tears, with a bedraggled "Abner" in the trunk of her car. Joyce sat in the lunchroom wondering what was making Mrs. Cartwright so ill-tempered. She had always been a perfectionist, but she had never been mean. Now she was taking her anger out on a plant!

Mrs. Cartwright came into the room without speaking, poured herself a cup of coffee, and sat down. Her face was tense, her mouth set in a firm line. Joyce felt awkward. What was she supposed to do? Suddenly, without warning, she felt compassion, an actual warmth, surge through her whole body. She looked up and said, "Mrs. Cartwright, are you feeling all right? Is everything going well at home?"

The response was abrupt. "As well as can be expected, I guess. Life is never easy."

The warm feeling would not go away. "I thought maybe something was wrong."

"And that's why I'm being hard on the girls? Are you playing psychologist?"

146

That hurt, but Joyce persisted. "No, I just wanted you to know I care. I think you're an excellent supervisor, and I'm not quitting, even though working here isn't the satisfaction that it used to be."

Mrs. Cartwright sat quietly, looking into her coffee cup. "You are very perceptive, Joyce. Things *aren't* going well at home. My husband is scheduled for eye surgery, with the probability that he'll have to find a different job. We still have two more children to put through college, and I'm feeling the pressure of being the chief wage-earner in the family."

That explained the rules and regulations in the office. Mrs. Cartwright was securing her hold on her own position!

The two women sat and talked a long time. Charlotte and Anne didn't come back to work, but Melanie did, bringing Abner in a new pot. He sprouted two leaves. It could have been the new pot, but Joyce liked to think it was the happier atmosphere.

> *O God, Thy judgments give the king,*
> *His reigning son Thy righteousness;*
> *He to Thy people right shall bring,*
> *With justice shall Thy poor redress.*
>
> *The heights shall bring prosperity,*
> *The hills bring peace by righteousness;*
> *He'll judge the poor, the wronged set free,*
> *And crush the men who them oppress.*
>
> Psalm 72:1–4

Whoever digs a pit may fall into it; whoever breaks through a wall may be bitten by a snake. Whoever quarries stones may be injured by them; whoever splits logs may be endangered by them (10:8–9).

In biblical times, digging a hole must have been a hazardous business. Both Psalms 7 and 57 mention the problem of falling in. Snakes were a common danger, being noted more than thirty times. Amos writes about a man entering his house, resting his hand on the wall, and being bitten (5:19). Felling trees was a skill in itself, and Solomon felt it necessary to call in the Sidonians to cut cedars for the temple. Stonemasons relied on flint tools. Huge blocks of stone were quarried by cutting a series of holes in the rock, driving wooden plugs into the holes and soaking them with water. The swelling would cause the rock to split.

The point of all this is that in any action there are risks. One can trip and break a hip just stepping outside to get the morning paper. We have to use our minds—and look ahead. As there is defensive driving, so is there defensive living. "Safety First" can be supported by Scripture!

The fear of accidents can cause us to draw back from involvement. A kind of paranoia sets in, and we seldom venture from our home. After a while, friends give up asking us to go out. They get tired of hearing about what *may* happen.

It is necessary to balance caution with risk. We are not to be foolhardy, but we are not to become recluses either. Older men and women are to be active in passing on the teaching and practice of the Christian faith (Titus 2). Pits and snakes are everywhere. We may think we can avoid them by staying home. It is wise to recall that the bitten man mentioned in Amos was resting in his own house.

But in a time accepted, LORD,
To Thee my prayers ascend;
In Thine abounding love and truth,
O God, salvation send.
Deliver me from out the mire,
And me from sinking keep;
Deliver me from those that hate,
And from the waters deep.

Let not the flood me overflow;
Let me not swallowed be
By gaping deep; let not the pit
Close up its mouth on me.
Because Thy mercy, LORD, is good,
O answer Thou my plea;
In all of Thy compassion great,
O turn Thou unto me.

Psalm 69:13–16

If the ax is dull and its edge unsharpened, more strength is needed but skill will bring success (10:10).

Think of yourself as an ax. You are a smoothly sanded, solid ash handle, with a solid forged-steel blade. A truly magnificent tool! The woodchopper picks you up, lifts you high above his head, and brings you down with all his strength, splitting an upright log into two pieces. His experienced feel for a good cut tells him that your edge is dull. If he is to maximize your usefulness, he must strike harder and perhaps tilt the blade slightly.

In the hands of a skilled axman you can still chop wood, but your effectiveness would be doubled if your blade were sharp. Oh, if he could only whet the edge, honing it until it cut through wood as if it were butter! How much easier the work would be!

The cutting edge of the Christian faith is prayer. This is what we are to do without ceasing (1 Thess. 5:17). This is what we cease doing so easily because it is repetitious, we are too tired, it seems ineffectual, or everything else needs to be done first. We don't pray, and life isn't much different. There are good days and bad days, successes and failures. We can skip prayer meeting and private devotions with little effect. The wood gets cut, eventually.

Like cutting with a dull ax, we can't know the difference until we try the same task with a sharp blade. We can't know the difference prayer makes until we pray regularly and purposefully. God's promises take effect after we have proceeded, by faith, to lift the ax.

Attend Thou and answer; Jehovah, give ear;
I, needy and poor, make my plea;
Preserve Thou my soul; save Thy servant, O God,
For godly and trusting is he.

Since all the day long do I cry unto Thee,
Show mercy, O Lord, unto me.
The soul of Thy servant cause Thou to rejoice;
I lift up my soul unto Thee.

Thou, Lord, dost show mercy; forgiving Thou art;
Abundant Thy kindness and love
To those who sincerely upon Thee do call.
My voice, Lord, attend from above.

Psalm 86:1–6

If a snake bites before it is charmed, there is no profit for the charmer (10:11).

The writer of Ecclesiastes has inserted into chapter 10 a few "pithy proverbs" to jolt us out of our complacency. Here he uses the example of a snake charmer—a familiar sight in the ancient culture of the Middle East.

The snake generally was a cobra, whose venom is deadly. Some charmers removed the fangs of their snakes, but we assume that in this case the charmer did not. It is essential, therefore, if he is to collect any coins from the crowd, that he mesmerize the snake by his rhythmic movements and then return it to its cage. The crowd is not going to pay money to see the man get bitten—but what would it matter, since he would surely die from the poison? There is a little Eastern humor here, which we should enjoy just as the early readers of Ecclesiastes did.

The point is that help is useless if it comes too late. The help is not so much the first aid administered in an emergency as it is the assistance given so that control is maintained and no emergency arises. When a friend's car shows signs of engine trouble, we can either take an hour off and make the necessary repair or else allow the car to break down on the interstate at midnight and be forced to drive out and pick her up. Preventive maintenance is the principle.

Another interpretation of this proverb is the need to bridle our tongue, described by James as "a restless evil, full of deadly poison" (3:8). If we regard the snake bite as a destructive conversation, the application is the same. Far better to prevent the words from being spoken than to offer medical help after the wound has been inflicted.

My heart doth overflow;
A noble theme I sing.
My tongue's a skilful writer's pen
To speak about the king.

More fair than sons of men
Thy lips with grace o'erflow,
Because His blessing evermore
Did God on thee bestow.

Thy sword gird on Thy thigh,
O Thou supreme in might,
And gird Thyself with majesty
And with Thy splendor bright.

Psalm 45:1–3

If a man is lazy, the rafters sag; if his hands are idle, the house leaks (10:18).

This is the kind of verse a wife likes to stick on the refrigerator door so her husband will be reminded to fix the light on the front porch. But while it could be handy to motivate the handyman, it is really in a context intended for kings. The house with its sagging rafters is a nation governed by an indolent ruler. He and his subordinates start partying early in the day and neglect their responsibilities.

Taking a broader view, we see that doing nothing can be as sinful as doing something wrong. Idleness allows our houses—nation, church, business, family—to fall into disrepair. Each of these spheres of life demands a constant, prayerful attention to detail. We need to keep informed of their needs so that we can make an appropriate beneficial response. The morning paper, missionary bulletin, office bulletin board, and family letter all demand our time.

We can also learn from this proverb that doing nothing makes us more vulnerable to doing something wrong. "Idleness is the devil's workshop," the saying goes. When we are not occupied in the Lord's work, the temptation arises to become involved in evil enterprises. Idleness leads to gossip, Paul points out in 1 Timothy 5:13. In his second letter to the Thessalonians, Paul links idleness with becoming a burden to other people and making us receptive to false pride (3:6ff.).

Retirement can be an excuse to withdraw from active ministry and spend the summer in some vacation retreat where the Lord's Day, the Lord's people, and the house of the Lord's people are completely forgotten. Overeating and drinking become the common lifestyle.

Sociologists report that in our later years we can become slovenly about our personal appearance and habits, lead-

154

ing to a destruction of sexual interest and response. Our own sexuality loses its appeal. If one marriage partner still cares about good grooming and manners, the temptation exists to begin a fresh sexual relationship with someone who feels a similar responsibility.

Whether our rafters or our abdominal muscles are sagging, Scripture calls us to make repairs.

According to the days we spent
Beneath affliction Thou hast sent,
And all the years we evil knew,
Now make us glad, our joy renew.
Thy work in all Thy servants show;
Thy glory on their sons bestow.

On us let there be shed abroad
The beauty of the LORD our God.
Our handiwork upon us be
Established evermore by Thee.
Yes, let our handiwork now be
Established evermore by Thee
Psalm 90:15–17

A feast is made for laughter, and wine makes life merry, but money is the answer for everything (10:19).

If money is the answer for everything, what is the question?

Money, we know, cannot ensure health, happiness, or immortality. It cannot buy peace of conscience or loving relationships. Yet it is not to be despised. Money supplies a thousand advantages. It can support a Christian college, send a missionary to Africa, supply Bibles for China, buy cooling fans for poor people in the city.

It is not money that is "a root of all kinds of evil," but the *love* of money (1 Tim. 6:10). Jesus condemns money when it becomes an object of devotion equal to God (Matt. 6:24). In His parable of the ten minas (Luke 19:11–26), the third servant who laid his money away in a piece of cloth was punished because he didn't put his money to work. He didn't even invest it so it could earn a little interest.

God is the ultimate supplier of all wealth. He puts us in a position where we have money, either by giving us employment, an inheritance, wise investments, or perhaps a jackpot because we matched picture cards from a fast-food restaurant. However we got what money we have, God enabled us to have it. Therefore, He has a right to say what we do with the money He gave us.

The question is, What is my most versatile possession? The answer is, Money. God's guideline to those who possess it is amazingly simple: "Command them to do good" (1 Tim. 6:18).

> "I'll take no calf nor goat
> From house or fold of thine;
> For cattle on a thousand hills
> And all wild beasts are Mine.

"The birds of mountains great
   Are all to Me well known;
The beasts that roam the field untamed,
   They, too, are all My own.

"Then if I hungry were
   I would not tell it thee,
Because the world with all its wealth
   Belongest unto Me."

Psalm 50:11–15

Do not revile the king even in your thoughts, or curse the rich in your bedroom, because a bird of the air may carry your words, and a bird on the wing may report what you say (10:20).

It has been said that rulers have a sixth sense for dissidents. Among the abilities that got them the position in the first place must be a discernment of character. Not that rulers are never blind. Through the ages, kings and presidents have been fooled. David erred in his trust of Joab. Alexandra's protection of Rasputin altered the course of Russian history. The "yes men" of recent American presidents have given bad advice. Generally speaking, though, rulers know who their enemies are.

God calls us to the very difficult task of not reviling the king, even in our thoughts. Surely in our bedroom we ought to be free to say what we really think about the president of the United States! God says no. We may not revile him—denounce him with abusive language—even in our own home. We may not harbor evil thoughts against the person in office even in our heads! When you've been active in politics or a party member of long standing, this is very hard to do.

Rather, we are to pray for those in authority, submit to governmental regulation, and protest only out of respect. Peter told the early church it was not to despise authority. His divinely inspired direction came during the reign of the Herodian kings—a family whose reputation for sins of the grossest sort was publicly known. Paul demanded his civil rights, but never out of a rebellious spirit.

Political activism is a field of service that many older citizens are finding fruitful. The 16 percent of our population that is over sixty has considerable clout among state and federal legislators. Within this group, Christians are making their distinctive impact. For us there are special guidelines, first stated in the time of Moses: "Do not curse the ruler of your people" (Exod. 22:28). This is reinforced by Paul in Acts 23:5 and exemplified by the leaders of the early church.

Give ear to what is right, O LORD!
O listen to my cry!
Give heed to this my earnest prayer
From lips which do not lie.

May judgment from Your presence come
Which will me vindicate,
And always may Your searching eyes
See what is just and straight.

For you have scrutinized my heart;
You came to me by night.
You've probed and found no ill intent;
My mouth speaks only right.

Psalm 17:1–3

Cast your bread upon the waters, for after many days you will find it again. Give portions to seven, yes to eight, for you do not know what disaster may come upon the land (11:1–2).

Whether the "bread" to be cast is bread-corn thrown on the receding waters of the Nile River so that it will imbed itself in a fertile river bank, or a merchant ship sent to exchange cargo at a distant port, the point is the same: Charity will never make us poor. Whatever we give away will come back to us a hundredfold in one form or another. Jesus made this principle one of His key teachings when He said, "Give, and it will be given to you. A good measure, pressed down, shaken together and running over, will be poured into your lap. For with the measure you use, it will be measured to you" (Luke 6:38).

Liberality requires a degree of risk. I may make a large donation to my church today and lose my job tomorrow. The investments I bequeath to a denominational agency can be worthless if the stock market crashes. While delivering food baskets to the poor, I can fall and crack my elbow.

It is true: We do not know what will happen. All the more reason why charity must be accompanied by faith. We must believe that God is going to give to us because we gave, and so that we may give again. Casting implies throwing with a certain amount of abandonment. We do not cast clothes into the laundry hamper. Pitchers do not cast balls to catchers. In those cases the receptor is known. Rather, we cast fishing lures or votes. In the Bible there are frequent references to casting lots; the outcome isn't sure until the action is taken.

This passage assumes we have some bread to cast. Somewhere along the way we were given resources and the charge to manage them wisely. You may have more to manage than I, but our responsibility to be judicious stewards is the same. God's promise is to us both: "He who is

160

kind to the poor lends to the LORD, and he will reward him
for what he has done" (Prov. 19:17).

> *How blessed the man who guides the poor*
> *By counsel strong and clear;*
> *The LORD will surely rescue him*
> *When evil days draw near.*
> *The LORD will guard him in the land;*
> *His life is blessed indeed;*
> *Nor will You let him fall before*
> *His adversaries' greed.*
>
> Psalm 41:1–2

Whoever watches the wind will not plant; whoever looks at the clouds will not reap (11:4).

Visit any church that has just erected a new sanctuary, and you can find someone who thinks they should have waited until the membership was larger. Attend any congregational meeting, and you'll hear someone speak against expanding the missions budget until the economy improves. We can always wait for a better time to do something, whether it's a project at church or a project at home, like fixing the patio.

In reality there are no ideal conditions for doing anything. Wind and clouds are going to come along to test our faith at one stage or another. When God directs us to act, our duty is to obey and leave the results to God. A young pastor and his wife who moved into a city neighborhood described as "hopeless for evangelism" were used to build a ministry that included a church, store, restaurant, and youth center. Now they have expanded to sponsor a mission church.

We are to plant. We take into account the weather, of course, and do not expect orange trees to thrive in Minnesota. Planting cannot be divorced from reality, so we suit the seed to its environment. Albert Schweitzer built a hospital in Gabon, West Africa, not a university.

As we become older, it is easy to fantasize. Either we imagine all sorts of difficulties that never happen, or else we sit in a reverie and build castles in the air. "Oh, if I were younger, what I would do!" God calls us to stop looking at the weather vane and get to work. As He is in charge of the wind and the clouds, so is He also the Lord of the harvest.

*From heav'n O praise the L*ᴏʀᴅ; *ye heights His glory raise.*
All angels, praise accord; let all His host give praise.
Praise Him on high, sun, moon, and star,
Ye heav'ns afar and cloudy sky.

Yea, let them glorious make Jehovah's matchless name;
For when the word He spake they into being came.
And from that place where fixed they be,
By His decree they cannot pass.

*From earth O praise the L*ᴏʀᴅ, *ye deeps and all below;*
Wild winds that do His word, ye clouds, fire, hail, and snow;
Ye mountains high, ye cedars tall,
Beasts great and small, and birds that fly.

Psalm 148:1–10

163

Sow your seed in the morning, and at evening let not your hands be idle, for you do not know which will succeed, whether this or that, or whether both will do equally well (11:6).

A radio talk show featured directors of two state farm bureaus. Much time had been given to the hazards of agriculture—the weather, insects, price fluctuations, governmental regulation, changing food habits. "With all these things going against farming," the radio announcer asked, "why does anyone keep on doing it?" The answer was immediate. "Farmers like to farm. They like the work, the challenge, the emphasis on family and home, being outdoors, working for themselves. It's a wonderful life, for all its problems, and they wouldn't be happy doing anything else."

Can we as Christian seed-sowers be happy doing anything else? Do we think ours is a wonderful life, for all its problems? Paul tells us in Ephesians to make "the most of every opportunity, because the days are evil" (5:16). Growing conditions aren't any better today than in the first century. In 2 Timothy 4:2 Paul writes, "Preach the Word; be prepared in season and out of season" (all the time). The thorns and rocks that inhibit God's Word from flourishing exist in the twentieth century, just as they did when Paul lived. In no age, at no age, has spreading the gospel been easy.

In the midst of uncertainty, we redouble our efforts. Right where we are, now, we sow seed, trusting God for the results. Paul says, "Remember this: Whoever sows sparingly will also reap sparingly, and whoever sows generously will also reap generously" (2 Cor. 9:6). You don't have to put in two hundred acres of corn to know that; a package of radish seeds will teach the same principle.

The young say they will wait until they are more mature

before they sow seed. The old say seed-sowing should be left to those who have more vigor. God says the age of the farmer isn't the important thing—it's getting the seed into the ground.

> The LORD brought Zion's exiles back.
> We were as men that dreamed.
> Our tongue was filled with melody;
> Our mouth with laughter teemed.
>
> "The LORD has done great things for them,"
> The heathen were agreed.
> The LORD has done great things for us,
> And we rejoice indeed!
>
> O LORD, as streams revive the south,
> Our exile band restore.
> Then those that sow their seed in tears
> Shall reap with joy once more.
>
> Though bearing forth the precious seed
> The reaper sowing grieves,
> He doubtless shall return again
> And bring with joy his sheaves.
>
> Psalm 126

Light is sweet, and it pleases the eyes to see the sun. How-
ever many years a man may live, let him enjoy them all. But
let him remember the days of darkness, for they will be
many. Everything to come is meaningless (11:7–8).

Can you really say that life is sweet? No matter what happened in the past, is it sweet right now? When you look out the bedroom window to see what the weather is like, do you rejoice that you have another day to live?

In her book *So Who's Afraid of Birthdays?* Anna Mow (at seventy-six) writes about the secret of a happy life. She points out that many people find a sense of fulfillment in church activities and service, but when that activity ceases, they feel lost and unwanted. All their lives their Christianity has been based upon the values of fellowship and mutual concern, but these "are simply not enough when the hardest trials of life come. Mere membership in a church is not enough to insure a healthy spiritual life."

The secret is a personal relationship with Jesus Christ. To the Colossians Paul wrote that God had commissioned him to present the Word of God in its fullness—"the mystery that has been kept hidden for ages and generations, but is now disclosed to the saints. To them God has chosen to make known among the Gentiles the glorious riches of this mystery, which is Christ in you, the hope of glory" (1:25–27).

Anna Mow continues: "A 'faith' that is only doctrinal belief may give security for a time, but the time may come when one feels he has to *hold* his faith. Whenever anyone gets protective of his faith, he gets hard and unloving. Such 'faith' brings no witness to the love of God. In definition it may be all right, but definitions can leave one cold and lonely."

If your life is sour, it may be because your faith has been in the church or in other people. Allow Christ to live in

166

your heart. He will fill you "to the measure of all the fullness of God" (Eph. 3:19). Your eyes will find pleasure in the morning sun.

> *Praise Jehovah; praise the Lord;*
> *Ye His servants, praise accord;*
> *Blessed be Jehovah's name;*
> *Evermore His praise proclaim.*
>
> *From the dawn to setting sun,*
> *Praise the Lord, the Mighty One.*
> *O'er all nations He is high;*
> *Yea, His glory crowns the sky.*
>
> *Who is like the Lord our God?*
> *High in heav'n is His abode,*
> *Who Himself doth humble low*
> *Things in heav'n and earth to know.*
>
> **Psalm 113:1–6**

Be happy, young man, while you are young, and let your heart give you joy in the days of your youth. Follow the ways of your heart and whatever your eyes see, but know that for all these things God will bring you to judgment (11:9).

A young man received a car on his twenty-first birthday. Incredulous, he asked his father, "Is it all mine?"

"Yes, it's all yours," he was assured.

"I can do whatever I want with it?"

"That's right," his father said.

Filled with excitement and power, the young man got into his new car and discovered that he couldn't get the ignition to work. There was a special device for inserting the key. He sat in the front seat and read the manual. Once he understood the function of all the dials and switches on the dashboard, he drove the car around town, picking up his friends and giving them rides.

As he was turning down Market Street, the engine gave a strange coughing sound and stopped, right in the middle of traffic. He had run out of gas! The policeman who came by to see what was causing all the trouble helped him push the car to the side of the road. He asked if the car's insurance included a charge for towing. Insurance? No one had said anything about insurance!

Ten gallons of gas later, the young man drove his car into his own driveway. He collected all the cups and napkins that littered the back seat. Someone had spilled root beer on the beautiful new upholstery. A smudge of dirt ran across the carpet. Sitting two deep in the back seat had caused hair oil to rub into the ceiling. It was going to take a lot of work to get the car looking new again.

He went into the house to find some cleaning fluid and a cloth.

"Phone for you!" his mother called out. He picked up the receiver.

"Hi! It's me—Phil!" the voice said. "A bunch of us guys were thinking it would be a blast to drive over to Hillsboro tonight and take in the rodeo. Since you have a new car, we were wondering, will you drive?"

For You will not give up my soul to the grave.
Your Holy One You will preserve from decay.
The pathway of life You will show unto me;
In Your glorious presence is fullness of joy.
Your right hand holds pleasures for me evermore.
                                    Psalm 16:10–11

So then, banish anxiety from your heart and cast off the troubles of your body, for youth and vigor are meaningless (11:10).

Think back to Ecclesiastes 3:11: "He has made everything beautiful in its time." Youth *is* beautiful in its time. We can't deny the envy we feel when we see supple bodies, smooth skin, and naturally colored hair. Young lovers have a special appeal. The way their bodies touch is electric. The spark of excitement can be felt by other people.

In our country, the attempt to retain the attributes of youth is a costly, ongoing experience that borders on desperation. We must appear to be thirty forever. The task that was formerly left to cosmeticians has been taken over by plastic surgeons, whose patients unabashedly display their handiwork. Sensible dieting has given way to self-inflicted starvation. Anorexia is receiving national attention.

In this verse we are told that youth and vigor are meaningless. Not that we shouldn't enjoy them while we can: we also read here that we should be happy while we are young. But youth is not to be idolized. We are not Peter Pans who never age. Don't be anxious about growing older, Koheleth says. Rejoice that you are growing!

> But like the palm tree flourishing
> Shall be the righteous one;
> He shall like to the cedar grow
> That is in Lebanon.
> Those that within Jehovah's house
> Are planted by His grace,
> They shall grow up and flourish all
> In our God's holy place.
>
> And in old age when others fade
> Their boughs with fruit shall bend;
> They shall be green and flourishing,

Their life in vigor end.
To show that upright is the LORD;
He is a rock to me,
And He from all unrighteousness
Is altogether free.

Psalm 92:12–15

*Remember your Creator in the days of your youth, before
the days of trouble come and the years approach when you
will say, "I find no pleasure in them" (12:1).*

G. B. Shaw said, "Youth is a wonderful thing; what a crime
to waste it on children." Life seems so much simpler, so
much more carefree, when we are just starting out. It is
possible on a moment's notice to pack a picnic lunch and
head for the beach. A few years later, such an impulse is
thwarted by errands and appointments that crowd out any
free time.

In our youth we are commanded to remember our Creator. *Remember.* Not suddenly remind ourselves that God
made us, but rather reflect on the Creation and all its im-
plications. We think of how God created everything, and us
in particular. Creation preceded sin in the world and resulted in salvation through Jesus Christ. It is imperative
that we work out the advancement of His kingdom before
the days come when we can no longer work.

There is also a sense of remembering constantly. David
says in Psalm 16:8, "I have set the LORD always before me.
Because he is at my right hand, I will not be shaken." The
fact that God created me permeates everything I think and
do. I am a unique handiwork, reflecting the glory of my
Originator. I am secure and confident in His protecting
love.

But suppose you are now experiencing years without
pleasure. Either you did not know God when you were
young, or you rejected Him then. You find no joy, no peace
in your present way of life. It all seems so meaningless, just
as the writer of Ecclesiastes says. Are you too old to find
God?

The prophet Jonah found himself facing his final hours.
He was inside a fish, engulfed by threatening water, sunk
down to the roots of the mountains. Life appeared to be

over. He prayed, "When my life was ebbing away, I remembered you, LORD, and my prayer rose to you, to your holy temple" (2:7). Jonah's distress was more than physical. He had been rebellious and felt banished from God's sight. "Those who cling to worthless idols forfeit the grace that could be theirs. But I, with a song of thanksgiving, will sacrifice to you. What I have vowed I will make good. Salvation comes from the LORD" (2:8-9).

God heard Jonah's prayer and promptly caused the fish to vomit him onto dry land. God will respond to any sincere prayer of repentance. It is never too late to experience His salvation. After years of floundering in deep waters, you can know the joy of a firm footing.

Praise waits for Thee in Zion! To Thee vows paid shall be.
O God of prayer the hearer, all flesh shall come to Thee.
Iniquities are daily prevailing over me,
But all of our transgressions are covered o'er by Thee.

Thou crownest years with goodness; Thy steps enrich the ground.
The desert pastures blossom; the hills with joy resound.
The fields with flocks are covered; the vales with grain are clad.
They all rejoice with shouting! They all with songs are glad!

Psalm 65:1-3, 11-13

... Before the sun and the light and the moon and the stars grow dark, and the clouds return after the rain; when the keepers of the house tremble, and the strong men stoop, when the grinders cease because they are few, and those looking through the windows grow dim ..." (12:2–3).

Our writer uses poetic imagery to describe old age. Our sensitivity grows dull. Legs and arms aren't steady. Our teeth fall out. Our eyes require stronger and stronger glasses, perhaps an operation for cataracts. All the marvels or geriatric medicine cannot forestall the effects of time.

We are told to remember our Creator before this happens. According to recent research, these physical effects will not be experienced by most people until they are past seventy-five. Some people won't feel them until they are around ninety. If you are sixty as you read this book, you have at least fifteen years to remember your Creator. Think what you can do in fifteen years!

In his letter to the Colossian church, Paul says to make the most of every opportunity. The King James Bible calls it "redeeming the time" (4:5). Paul gives specific instruction for how this can be done: "Devote yourselves to prayer.... Be wise in the way you act toward outsiders.... Let your conversation be always full of grace, seasoned with salt, so that you may know how to answer everyone" (Col. 4:2, 5–6).

Isn't it reassuring—yes, exciting!—to know that we can follow everyone of these instructions even though we have poor eyes, trembling hands, and false teeth? Truly we are never too old to serve God!

> LORD, in Thy tent who will abide with Thee,
> And on Thy holy hill a dweller be?
>   Who walks in uprightness,
>   Who worketh righteousness,
> Who doth the truth express unfeignedly;

Whose tongue doth not defame nor harm his friend,
Who to his neighbor's shame no ear doth lend,
Who has the vile abhorred
But honor doth accord
To those who fear the LORD and Him attend.

When to his hurt he swears naught changes he;
His gold no increase bears from usury;
His hands no bribes receive
The guiltless to aggrieve.
Lo, he who thus doth live unmoved shall be.

Psalm 15

When men are afraid of heights and of dangers in the streets; when the almond tree blossoms and the grasshopper drags himself along and desire no longer is stirred. Then man goes to his eternal home and mourners go about the streets (12:5).

The day comes when traveling, even if it is only to a department store, is difficult and dangerous. You can be too slow to cross the street before the light turns red. Or you can trip on the stairs. Escalators are risky. Elevators take your breath away. You don't have your former pep, either. Why do shopping centers have so few benches?

Life at home reaches a plateau of sexual apathy. Medical studies show that passion can continue all of one's life, but for many people it becomes an effort to get aroused. So a man at eighty fathered his thirteenth child—his wife was forty-two.

Here is this deteriorating body, with its faltering mind, and our poet puts it all under a blossoming almond tree— the first tree in the Holy Land to bloom in winter. Its very name in Hebrew means "waker" or "watcher." That isn't white hair up there on our head, that's beautiful flowers! Maybe we wouldn't drag ourselves around so much if we acted as if we were an almond tree, awake and watching.

When it came to the effects of old age, Paul could empathize. He suffered years of poor health, endured physical abuse, and bore up under many disappointments and sorrows. He had aches and pains, but he also had hope. To the church at Corinth he wrote, "Now we know that if the earthly tent we live in is destroyed, we have a building from God, an eternal house in heaven, not built by human hands.... For while we are in this tent, we groan and are burdened, because we do not wish to be unclothed but to be clothed with our heavenly dwelling, so that what is mortal may be swallowed up by life. Now it is God who has made us for this very purpose and has given us the Spirit as a deposit, guaranteeing what is to come" (2 Cor. 5:1, 4–5).

What is to come? We will be in heaven, at home with our Lord. That's what we are watching for, we who have heads covered with almond blossoms.

> *O Jehovah, hear my words;*
> *To my thoughts attentive be.*
> *Hear my cry, my King, my God,*
> *For I make my prayer to Thee.*
> *With the morning light, O LORD,*
> *Thou shalt hear my voice and cry;*
> *In the morn my prayer arrange*
> *And keep constant watch will I.*
>
> Psalm 5:1–3

Remember him—before the silver cord is severed, or the golden bowl is broken; before the pitcher is shattered at the spring, or the wheel broken at the well; and the dust returns to the ground it came from, and the spirit returns to God who gave it (12:6–7).

The allusion here is to a bowl, filled with oil, suspended by chains from the ceiling. Not too different from the hanging lamps that are popular today. Other containers mentioned in these verses are a clay pitcher and a bucket that could be lowered into a well.

We are all fragile containers. Within our bodies dwells the spirit of life. A day will come when our bodies will break, just like a clay pitcher, and that spirit will return to God. He will assign it to a final resting place, either in heaven or hell. If we have known God as Lord and Savior, our spirit resides with Him. Fanny Crosby writes of this in the hymn "Saved by Grace":

> "Someday the silver cord will break,
> And I no more as now shall sing;
> But O the joy when I shall wake
> Within the palace of the King!"

The Teacher tells us to remember our Creator before the silver cord is broken. He speaks to those who have never acknowledged God as Lord of their lives. They have no assurance of heaven, no anticipation that they will wake up in the palace of the King. Death is the fearful consequence of a life devoted to satisfying oneself. Everything, at last, has proven to be utterly meaningless. The body returns to the ground as dust, as dry and withered grass. The spirit suffers endless torment, darkness, weeping, gnashing of teeth.

It is never too late to come to God. Nor is it ever too late to be a witness for Him. At a time in our lives when we are tempted to withdraw from the maelstrom of Christian activity and sit by our fireplaces and television sets, we find our contemporaries open to the gospel. Death is imminent and certain. The good news of eternal life can be good news indeed.

Whether we acknowledge it or not, life hangs by a cord. When it breaks, and the golden bowl is shattered, the spirit must find another resting place. When we have the assurance of heaven, we can help others who are about to break.

> The LORD is my shepherd; no want shall come nigh.
> Within the green pastures He makes me to lie.
> Beside the still waters He leads me to rest;
> My soul He revives when I'm faint and oppressed.
>
> In right ways He leads me for His own name's sake.
> Although through the vale of death's shadow I walk,
> Since You are there with me, no evil I fear;
> Your rod and Your staff give me comfort and cheer.
>
> You set me a table before all my foes.
> My head You anoint, and my cup overflows.
> Your goodness and mercy attend my life's ways;
> I'll dwell in the house of the LORD endless days.
>
> Psalm 23

The words of the wise are like goads, their collected sayings like firmly embedded nails—given by one Shepherd. Be warned, my son, of anything in addition to them. Of making many books there is no end, and much study wearies the body (12:11–12).

The last part of this passage is popular with college students at the end of the semester. Koheleth is not talking just about textbooks, however, but of all books that purport to be the "words of the wise"—treatises on the meaning of life. "Look at the Holy Scriptures," he says, "which come from the one Shepherd, Jesus. They contain the wisdom that nails down eternal truths."

There are thousands of books that claim to be the truth. The collected philosophies of men down through the ages would fill several warehouses. Every cult has its leader who claims to possess special insight. Then there is the institutionalized church, which accepts Scripture but adds to it extraneous material that is entirely out of the minds of ecclesiastical mortals. To study all this literature is indeed wearying.

One of the most amazing facts about the Bible is that it is *portable*. Have you ever thought about this? All that God wants us to know about Him is in a book we can carry in our hand! We don't have to spend a thousand dollars for a set of encyclopedias or journey to a special library where a million volumes are stored. The meaning isn't so difficult that we have to have an advanced education. The Bible can be thoughtfully read in a year or less.

God wants us to know Him. He has made this information accessible to anyone who has the desire. All the knowledge we need for life and godliness has been made easily available. Peter writes, "He has given us his very great and precious promises, so that through them you may participate in the divine nature and escape the corruption in

180

this world caused by evil desires" (2 Peter 1:4).

To study the promises of God is not wearying. Instead they lead us to repentance and cause us to turn to God; our spirits are refreshed (Acts 3:19). We think again of our Good Shepherd who restores our soul. He has given us all the words we need to make our lives pleasing to Him.

O how I love Thy law; it is my study all the day.
It makes me wiser than my foes; its precepts with me stay.
More than my teachers or the old Thy servant understands;
Thy testimonies I consult and follow Thy commands.

I stayed my feet from evil ways that I Thy word observe;
I have been taught by Thee and from Thy judgments will not
swerve.

How sweet in taste Thy promises, than honey far more sweet!
Thy precepts understanding give; I therefore hate deceit.

Psalm 119:97–104

Now all has been heard; here is the conclusion of the matter;
Fear God and keep his commandments, for this is the whole
duty of man. For God will bring every deed into judgment,
including every hidden thing, whether it is good or evil
(12:13–14).

When we talk about fearing God, we like to equate it with
"having a reverence for" or "being in awe of." We are not
comfortable with its real meaning: "to dread." We nurture
the image of God as a heavenly Father who may disapprove
of what we are doing but won't spank us very hard, because
His love for us blinds Him to our real faults.

This is not what the Bible teaches. "For we must all appear before the judgment seat of Christ, that each may
receive what is due him for the things done in the body,
whether good or bad" (2 Cor. 5:10). "My eyes are on all their
ways; they are not hidden from me, nor is their sin con-
cealed from my eyes," says the Lord in Jeremiah 16:17. "But
I tell you that men will have to give account on the day of
judgment for every careless word they have spoken," says
Jesus in Matthew 12:36.

The prospect of having everything I have ever thought,
said, or done exposed to God does fill me with dread. It
drives me to ask His forgiveness. "O LORD, have mercy on
me; heal me, for I have sinned against you" (Ps. 41:4). God
graciously pardons me through the shed blood of Jesus
Christ. My sins are covered over. God remembers them no
more (Heb. 10:17–18). How can I please God, who has been
so good to me? "Keep my commandments," He says over
and over again. This is my whole duty. This makes my life
purposeful.

We may recoil at a God who knows so much and expects
so much. Even though He also gives us the power of the
Holy Spirit to enable us, we may draw back at such a high
standard. If only God were a little more loose, a little more

casual! But if He were, the loss would be ours. A God who overlooks would be a god who doesn't care.

That is not God. He cares for us. He loves us with an everlasting love; He has drawn us to Him with lovingkindness (Jer. 31:3). What we do is very important to Him. Nothing is meaningless when it is done to please God. This is the message of Ecclesiastes.

The LORD is just in His ways all;
In all His works His grace is shown;
The LORD is nigh to all that call,
Who call in truth on Him alone.

He will the just desire fulfill
Of such as do Him fear indeed;
Their cry regard and hear He will,
And save them in the time of need.

The LORD doth safely keep all those
Who bear to Him a loving heart,
But workers all of wickedness
Destroy will He and clean subvert.

Then with my mouth and lips I will
Jehovah's name with praise adore.
And let all bless His holy name
Forever and for evermore.

Psalm 145:17–21